The challenge of
teaching
controversial issues

The challenge of teaching
controversial issues

W

The challenge of teaching controversial issues

Edited by Hilary Claire and Cathie Holden

Trentham Books

Stoke on Trent, UK and Sterling, USA

Trentham Books Limited
Westview House   22883 Quicksilver Drive
734 London Road   Sterling
Oakhill   VA 20166-2012
Stoke on Trent   USA
Staffordshire
England ST4 5NP

© 2007 Hilary Claire and Cathie Holden

First published 2007

British Library Cataloguing-in-Publication Data
A catalogue record for this book is available from the British Library

ISBN: 978 1 85856 415 9

Cover illustration by Harriet Seddon

Designed and typeset by Trentham Print Design Ltd,
Chester, UK and printed in Great Britain by Cromwell Press Ltd,
Trowbridge

Contents

Dedications

For Thembi, a tribute to your courage in controversial and difficult situations and determination to get at the truth – Hilary

For Uncle Tom, with thanks – Cathie

The Contributors

Kathy Bickmore is Associate Professor at the Ontario Institute for Studies in Education, University of Toronto, Canada. She teaches graduate and pre-service teacher education and conducts research in education for constructive conflict, peace building, conflict resolution, equity, and citizenship/demo-cratisation in public school contexts. Her work has appeared in the *Handbook of Research in Social Studies, International Journal of Citizenship and Teacher Education, Journal of Peace Education, Canadian Journal of Education* (theme issue, Democracy and Education), and *Theory and Research in Social Educa-tion* (theme issue, Education for Peace Building Citizenship).

Paul Carr is from Toronto, Canada, and is presently Assistant Professor of Educational Foundations at Youngstown State University in Ohio, USA. His teaching and research interests lie in critical multiculturalism, democracy and social justice in education. He has been involved in antiracism work for many years, and has published on educational policy and diversity. He is co-editor of a forthcoming book on Whiteness in education.

Hilary Claire is a freelance writer, lecturer and consultant on History and Citizenship. She was brought up and educated in South Africa which has strongly informed her commitment to equality and democracy. She was a pri-mary teacher and deputy head in London, an advisory teacher in race and gender equality, and senior lecturer in history, education and citizenship on primary ITE courses. Publications include *Reclaiming our Pasts: equality and diversity in the primary history curriculum, Not Aliens: primary school children and the citizenship/PSHE curriculum, Teaching Citizenship in Primary Schools* and a memoir of growing up under apartheid *The Song Remembers When.*

Bernadette Dean is Associate Professor and head of academic and student affairs at Aga Khan University, Karachi, Pakistan. Her teaching and research interests are in social studies education, citizenship and human rights educa-tion, and teaching and learning in Pakistani schools. She has numerous pub-lications including social studies textbooks and a teaching learning resource to educate for citizenship, human rights and conflict resolution, and has pre-sented her research in national and international conferences.

Olwen Goodall is an educational psychologist who has taught across the primary age range in Devon and Somerset schools. She has been actively involved in the Teachers' Peace Education Network. Olwen has worked at the School of Education at Exeter University for fourteen years, most recently training Early Years teachers and co-ordinating the Early Years humanities course. Her research interests are in the area of social cognition in young children.

James Hennessy is Senior Lecturer at the College of St Mark and St John in Plymouth, UK where he is the Drama Programme Leader. James' background is as a professional actor and director working in community theatre. His PhD involved an examination of models of reflective practice used by actors when working within a Theatre-in-Education (TIE) context.

David Hicks is Professor in the School of Education at Bath Spa University. He is internationally recognised for his work on the need for a global and futures dimension in the curriculum and is particularly interested in ways of helping students and teachers think more critically and creatively about the future. His most recent books are *Lessons for the Future: The Missing Dimension in Education* and, with Cathie Holden, *Teaching the Global Dimension: Key Principles and Effective Practice*.

Cathie Holden is Associate Professor at the University of Exeter where she teaches on both primary humanities and secondary citizenship PGCE courses. Prior to this she taught in middle schools for 15 years. She is on the QCA working party for citizenship education and on the steering group of CitizED. She is currently researching children's understanding of local and global issues and their commitment to act for change. Books include: *Education for Citizenship: Ideas into Action* with Nick Clough and *Teaching the Global Dimension: Key Principles and Effective Practice* with David Hicks.

Andrew Hughes is Professor of Education at the University of New Brunswick in Canada. His particular interests lie in program evaluation and in the application of best practice research to teaching and learning in the social sciences. He is the author of more than 75 commissioned reports. His recent work in citizenship education has involved extensive collaboration with the Russian Association for Civic Education.

Norio Ikeno is Professor of Social Studies in the Faculty of Education at Hiroshima University, where he teaches curriculum and pedagogy on the secondary Teacher Education courses. He is vice president of the Japan Social Studies Association. His main research interests are international comparisons and new approaches to citizenship/social studies education. With colleagues in UK and Japan, Norio has inaugurated a comparative project on global citizenship in both countries.

Fran Martin is Senior Lecturer in education at the University of Exeter. Before moving into initial teacher education, she was an Early Years specialist, and an advisory teacher for the humanities. She specialises in geographical and environmental education, and has research interests in sustainable development, the global dimension and school partnerships. Fran has published extensively in all of these areas and is currently editor of the Geographical Association's journal, *Primary Geography*.

Debra Myhill is Professor of Education at the University of Exeter and is currently Head of Initial Teacher Education and course leader for PGCE secondary English. Her research interests focus principally on aspects of language and literacy teaching, including underachievement, equality issues, children's writing, and talk in the classroom. She writes regularly for the *Secondary English Magazine*. She is the author of *Better Writers* and of *Talking, Listening, Learning: Effective Talk in the Primary Classroom*.

Rahat Joldoshalieva teaches at Aga Khan University, Karachi, Pakistan. She is a member of the Citizenship Rights and Responsibilities Pakistan team which aims to train teachers, develop materials and conduct research in the areas of citizenship, human rights and peace education. Her research interests are in social citizenship and teacher development through action research. With Bernadette Dean she is currently conducting research on developing teachers' knowledge and skills for taking social action.

Alistair Ross is Professor of Education at London Metropolitan University, where he is Director of the Institute for Policy Studies in Education. He co-ordinates the European Thematic Network on Children's Identities and Citizenship in Europe. Formerly a primary teacher in inner London, his research interests include social justice and equity in education, the recruitment and careers of teachers, and the curriculum and political learning.

Alan Sears is Professor of Education at the University of New Brunswick in Canada. His research interests are related to citizenship education in Canada and internationally, with a particular focus on best practices for teaching and learning. He has written extensively in the field, including a recent co-authored book: *Neoliberalism, Globalisation and Human Capital Learning: Reclaiming Education for Democratic Citizenship*. He is Chief Regional Editor for Canada of the journal *Citizenship Teaching and Learning*.

Anne Sliwka is Professor of Education and Head of Teacher Education (Secondary Schools) at the University of Trier in Germany. Her current research focuses on school development and innovation, citizenship education and constructivist learning settings in secondary schools.

Manju Varma-Joshi taught a First Nations elementary class fourteen years ago. The obvious inequities in their education experiences ignited her interest in antiracist education. Since then she has earned a PhD in multicultural curriculum, worked as a classroom teacher, civil servant, curriculum designer, textbook reviewer and university professor, all in the area of multiculturalism. She has published several articles in national and international journals. She is president of Diversity Matters, a consulting business in diversity issues.

Ruth Versfeld works in South Africa on educational research, textbook development and inservice teacher education. A particular interest is in developing appropriate classroom methodologies for teaching and learning. Research topics include studying issues of multilingualism and language development for the Western Cape Department of Education and identifying cases of best practice within a range of educational contexts. Publications include textbooks for the new South African outcomes-based curriculum which address topics such as indigenous knowledge, teaching controversial issues and approaches to resisting racism in South African schools.

Part 1 – Overview and policy issues

The challenge of teaching controversial issues: principles and practice

Hilary Claire and Cathie Holden

A scene in a classroom in Torbay, November 2006

Fourteen children aged nine to eleven are sitting in a semi-circle. It is the last of three sessions on controversial issues. The children are giving presentations on topics they themselves have chosen as being controversial and which they have researched over the past month. They include:

- Should people be allowed to wear religious items at work or in public?

- Do we want a casino in Torbay?

- Should we encourage foreigners, like Bulgarians and Romanians, to come here?

- Should we ban smoking in public places?

- How can we solve the housing problem in the South West?

- Who's worth more: a footballer or a nurse?

The first topic, inspired by the recent decision of a primary school not to allow a Muslim teacher to wear her veil in the classroom, generates the following discussion:

Child 1: I think people should be allowed to wear religious items like a cross or a Jewish star or veil but I can understand how it would be hard to wear a veil and teach.

Child 2: Well, I think people shouldn't wear it, because no one can tell if they are happy or not or what they are feeling.

Teacher: I heard someone say that Britain is a Christian country and people should fit in.

Child 3: Well, my dad doesn't think she should wear it but I think she should because it's her religion.

Child 4: If we moved country, we wouldn't like it if we had to lose our religion.

Child 4: My headteacher thinks they should be allowed to do it but not if they are doing it to prove a point – like if he banned earrings and then someone wore cross earrings.

The children listen, consider the opinions of others, including their parents and teachers, and formulate their own ideas. The teacher inter-venes to challenge, to put another point of view, rather than to dominate the debate. She makes sure all children contribute and moves the discus-sion on at an appropriate point.

Introduction

As the example above demonstrates, children are aware of local and global controversial issues in the news. They can also understand the nature of controversy and debate the pros and cons with their peers. The level of discussion generated indicates the potential of such teaching not only for engaging children's interest but also for stimulating higher level dialogic debate (Wegerif, 2003) and fostering thinking skills. However, to have such reflective conversations, children require careful guidance, practice and skilled teaching. It is no accident that the teacher working with these children was highly experienced and confident, com-mitted to education for democratic citizenship.

This book has been compiled to help teachers feel confident to teach about controversial issues, to understand the nature of controversy and the value of teaching about such issues. In so doing they will be addressing children's concerns, helping them find non-violent solutions to current conflicts and preparing them for their future in an increasingly global and diverse society.

It is only recently that global and controversial issues have re-emerged onto the UK educational scene. The 1980s saw teaching about such issues come to a halt as teachers struggled to come to terms with the require-ments of the national curriculum. More recently, however, citizenship, race equality and sustainability have emerged as key areas of concern. Sir

Bernard Crick, the 'father' of the new citizenship curriculum, has argued that many young people are interested in particular political and controversial issues (e.g. animal rights, environmental issues, improving their local community) and that we need to equip them with 'the political skills needed to change laws in a peaceful and responsible manner' (QCA, 1998: 10). Effective teaching about controversial issues is at the heart of this:

> Controversial issues are important in themselves and to omit informing about and discussing them is to leave a wide and significant gap in the educational experience of young people. (QCA, 1998:56)

Guidance on the role of the teacher in teaching about controversial issues then followed from the QCA (1998, 2000), as did various booklets and teaching packs. Most notable is Fiehn (2005) which, while aimed at post 16 students, is relevant for all secondary students, and Garlake (2003) again for the secondary classroom. Our own work has focused on controversial issues in primary schools (Holden, *Teaching the tricky bits: topical, political and controversial issues*, 2002; Claire, *Dealing with controversial issues with primary teacher trainees*, 2003, and *Teaching Citizenship in the Primary School*, 2004). There is also support on the web, e.g. briefings on particular topical controversial issues from The Citizenship Foundation, (http://www.citizenshipfoundation.org.uk/main/page.php?92), specific advice on dealing with controversies arising from racism on www.Britkid.com and schemes of work on www.citized.info such as Arstall's on teaching secondary pupils about conflict resolution (http://www.citized.info/pdf/students/Laura_Arstall_SOW.pdf).

All the above, however, is in the form of booklets, articles or web resources. No book has been devoted solely to the teaching of controversial issues since the 1980s. We therefore felt it was timely to gather together good practice and the best thinkers in the field in a new publication. We wanted an international perspective: controversial issues are not the domain of the UK and there is much to be learnt from listening to others who are trying out effective strategies in their own countries. In particular we have tried to include voices from countries who are finding their way as democracies and in so doing have realised how similar the issues are for teachers all over the world.

Are young people concerned about controversial issues?
Our work in recent years has involved us both in listening to what young people have to say about their worlds and their concerns about the future. Claire's work in multi-ethnic inner London schools was published in 2001

in *Not Aliens: Primary School Children and the Citizenship/PSHE Curriculum*. The title came from an eleven year old Bengali boy, Ibrahim. When he was interviewed he spoke about the attitudes of white indigenous English children – and some teachers – who, he felt, saw children like himself as 'aliens', like monsters from outer space, not fully human, not belonging. The research reported in *Not Aliens* confirmed for us that children are part of the adult world – they fool about more, have a greater capacity to stay light hearted and are not necessarily as experienced and informed as older people, but they know about and care about much the same things as the adults in their family and community.

The interviews revealed just how much children absorb from the media, from the conversations they overhear even if they don't participate. The inner city children, whatever their ethnicity, talked with considerable knowledge and insight about racism, poverty, drug abuse, alcoholism, homelessness, crime, climate change, pollution, danger on the streets, child abuse. They know and think about relationships – between their parents, between different ethnic and cultural groups where they live, between different religious communities. In short, controversy is part of their everyday lives.

Our research in 2004/5 with over five hundred young people aged nine to fourteen endorsed the above. These pupils, from diverse areas across the south of England, were well aware of the problems in their communities and wanted less violence, less crime and fewer drunks, drug dealers and gangs. They were concerned to have more or cheaper housing and enough jobs. Children in inner-city London discussed the major controversies in their communities, in their countries of origin and the wider world. Iraq, terrorist bombings, religious fundamentalism and global warming came up time and again. All the pupils, whether from the inner cities or rural Devon, were aware of current global conflicts, especially Iraq, and wanted an end to wars, a solution to global poverty and more action on environmental issues. Furthermore they wished to learn about these issues at school so that they could understand them better and be proactive in working for change (Holden, 2007).

This study was extended in 2005/6 beyond the UK to nine other countries and the data from these children indicate that English children are not alone in their awareness of the wider world. The South African children, for example, were without exception thankful to have escaped the dreadful years of apartheid, but they were not unaware or unconcerned about the problems which apartheid had spawned. AIDS, crime, poverty, un-employment, drug abuse and the perverted prevalence of violent sexual crime directed at children were repeated concerns. In the small group interviews, they built on each other's discourses, but they also argued, sometimes vehemently. It is impossible to imagine that these children were innocent, indifferent to controversies in the wider world, or in-capable of discussing them.

This international research indicates that from South Africa to Kyrgyzstan, from the Ukraine to Spain, children fear increased conflict at home and abroad, more poverty and environmental degradation, whilst at the same time hoping that the future will be better. They are often only partially informed and want to know more. They are unsure of their own role but know that the issues are important and look to school to help them make sense of complexity and controversy (Holden *et al*, 2006).

What are controversial issues?

When one listens to children talk about their communities, local and global, it appears that they are aware of what we would consider the controversial issues of the day. But can we define this further? Is it merely what is in the news or is it more than this? If we go back to the work of Wellington (1986:3), he maintains that a controversial issue is one which a) is considered important by an appreciable number of people and b) involves value judgments, so that the issue cannot be settled by facts, evidence or experiment alone. Stradling adds that they are the issues that deeply divide a society and that generate conflicting explanations and solutions based on alternative value systems (Stradling *et al*, 1984). Richardson (1986:27) warns, however, that it is not just a case of 'people agree or they don't, society is divided or it isn't': the situation is more com-plex, as 'certain interests are served by maintaining that there is no contro-versy, no difference of opinion, no protest or discontent, that we're all one happy family. Conversely, certain other interests are served through the recognition that such and such an issue should be debated, should be on the agenda.' Thus the decision about what is seen as controversial is in itself controversial, as interest groups may work to stifle debate in order to maintain the *status quo* or, conversely, bring specific issues into the public arena in order to advance their cause. In general terms a controversial issue is one in which

■ the subject/area is of topical interest

5

- there are conflicting values and opinions
- there are conflicting priorities and material interests
- emotions may become strongly aroused
- the subject/area is complex

(adapted from Perry, 1999).

What controversial issues might be relevant for the classroom? As the re-search with children shows, local issues in the news such as housing and immigration can be debated, as can global issues such as damage to the environment or international conflict. Writing for a post-16 audience, Fiehn (2005:11) gives 'war, immigration, abortion, gay rights, the European Union' as examples of relevant controversial issues. The Citizenship Foundation provides briefings on topical controversial issues and in late 2006 offered source material for teachers on GM crops, hunting with hounds, identity cards, prisons, smoking in public places and reducing the voting age to 16. Oxfam's *Teaching Controversial Issues, Global Citizenship Guide* (2006) provides activities for primary children on diversity, peace and conflict resolution and social justice and equity.

Why teach about controversial issues now?

As we have discussed earlier, children's worlds are now full of controversial issues about which they care deeply. Dealing with such issues, seeing the local-global links and looking to the future requires teachers to have sensitivity and skill. Bland, formulaic responses or, even worse, pretending that the children neither know nor care about controversial issues, is patronising and potentially dangerous. We wouldn't dream of handing over a fast car to someone who didn't know how to drive. The controversial issues with which children wish to engage are potentially far more dan-gerous and they need education and strategies for managing them with-out violence.

It is not just that children and students encounter controversy in their communities and the wider world, every day of their lives, whether first hand or through the media; it is not just that they are worried and con-cerned. Hicks and Holden (1995) reminded us a decade ago that educa-tion must 'teach for tomorrow', not just for today. In the 1930s and 1940s, and in the 1950s through to the late 1980s, clashing ideologies polarised the world. Today, the leaders of the fascist and racist British National Party are met on the steps of a court with cheering followers and equally vocal hostility; today our national newspapers devote pages to warnings about the imminent catastrophes of climate change and about the depletion of fish in the oceans; today soldiers come back in body bags from Iraq and from Afghanistan. In the Middle East, parts of Africa, Latin America and South East Asia, violent conflicts over territory and ideology cause the deaths of civilians as well as soldiers. Emigration, which has always been one answer to economic uncertainty and political hazard, is not necessarily viewed positively by receiving countries, and leads to concomitant political and social tensions. Human rights are by no means guaranteed to everyone in our global village. We do not know what threats to peace, social justice and progress the next decades will bring – threats which our children will not just inherit, but must defuse. Knowing how to make sense of the arguments and how to move beyond knee jerk reactions, having the skills and strategies to deal with conflict are not just optional extras in their education, they are essential to the survival of their world.

Children have to learn to deal with such difference and controversy. They are not born knowing how to do this and need to practise skills of listening, stating their case, and being prepared to change their minds or rethink their values if necessary. Learning how to deal with sensitive controversial issues in a structured setting, through topics introduced into the classroom, can be a rehearsal for dealing with more immediate controversy in the playground, home or community. It is also part of preparation for living in a democratic society where controversial issues are debated and discussed without recourse to violence.

Is universal suffrage sufficient to resolve the controversies of the modern world?

In the nineteenth century many disenfranchised people believed that once everyone had the vote, citizens would exercise their views about controversial issues through the ballot box and democratic processes would ensure their solution. The democratic electoral system itself is premised on the idea of competing ideologies and policies: where it works well, rational debate on the hustings, in the media and in parliament itself should resolve conflict. The opportunity to debate controversial issues in a free and uncensored forum is generally accepted to be at the heart of democracy.

Since the late twentieth century assumptions about suffrage, voting and democracy within nation states have come under scrutiny. History suggests that the suffrage alone has not been enough to ensure democracy or the resolution of conflict and that citizens adopt a variety of strategies which go beyond the ballot box in attempting to engage constructively with controversy. In a climate of cynicism about politics and politicians, an increasing number of people abstain from using their vote anyway. In addition, the most urgent problems of our contemporary world are perceived to be global, not national – and democratic institutions were originally designed for smaller city and later nation states – not for the global context. In addition, even democratically elected, constitutional governments have appeared in recent years to override the will of the people when they engage with international controversies.

National elections may redress the situation, with voters removing from office politicians who have appeared to ignore widely-held public views. However, the global or multinational institutions which are set up to deal with trans-national matters – for example the EEC, African Union and Association of South East Asian Nations (ASEAN), the United Nations and its various departments, G8, the IMF, the World Trade Organisation – are not democratically elected bodies. Between elections, and where representative government is seen to be inadequate to the task of dealing with urgent global issues, conflict and controversy are typically addressed through one issue politics. These approaches are sometimes informally organised, and sometimes managed through NGOs. Web-based politics regularly bypasses the conventional democratic processes of representative governments and the issues are not always resolved peacefully. Young people still need to learn how to resolve conflict through the conventional democratic channels, if these are to maintain any credibility. But they also need to learn how to make sense of the issues and controversies which go beyond national democratic politics, and use the new methods of communication and organisation responsibly.

What are the concerns of teachers?

Recent research with teachers and Initial Teacher Education (ITE) students in Britain reveals a sense of inadequacy, a lack of training or of confidence in approaching controversial issues effectively with children and students of various ages. For example, a survey of 187 primary and secondary ITE students in Wales (Robbins *et al*, 2003) indicated that two thirds did not feel qualified for this role. Revell (2005) found that student teachers thought their training had been apolitical, 'overwhelmingly practical, concentrating on curriculum delivery' rather than requiring them to understand or question underlying issues. A national survey of 679 teachers (Davies *et al*, 1999) indicated that they had barely touched on

8

education for democracy or teaching about controversial issues. More-over, these teachers' views about citizenship education were overwhelm-ingly apolitical, seeing it not as the potential instrument for envisioning progressive change and resolving conflict but as 'meeting obligations'. Though this latter discourse encouraged communitarian ideals, there was no hint that in the face of racism, sexism and clashes of ideology and interests, the discharge of such obligations might, in reality, be fraught with controversy. These teachers thought that being on time, obeying school rules and picking up litter were signposts of effective citizenship education.

A report in 2004 (Oulton *et al*) confirmed that 'the vast majority' of 200 primary and secondary teachers interviewed had had no training in teaching controversial issues and felt they had insufficient guidance from the national curriculum or their schools. Only one in eight teachers felt well prepared to teach controversial issues. Research in the West Midlands (Hess, 2004) revealed that there was a mismatch between what pupils wanted with respect to controversial issues, and what teachers felt equip-ped and prepared to deal with. Teachers regularly indicated that they were anxious about the politically charged nature of controversy, were afraid of accusations of indoctrination and lacked the education and training to take on controversy in the classroom.

We may appreciate that teachers and students in ITE are not well equip-ped to teach about controversy, but forget that the values and attitudes held by some teachers may themselves be undemocratic. A survey in 2001 of 400 postgraduate ITE students in England revealed that 10 per cent held racist attitudes whilst others complained that antiracism or antisexism was 'shoved down their throats' (Wilkins, 2001). Research by Holden and Hicks (2007) found that undergraduate student teachers were much less predisposed than their PGCE counterparts to teach about global issues and less secure in their ability to do, and were likely to stick to 'safe' areas such as recycling rather than tackle what they saw as difficult issues. All student teachers, however, were concerned about their own role when teaching controversial global issues, the reaction of parents and appro-priate strategies for the classroom including how to deal with children's responses. In short they needed much more guidance and support than was available on any of their pre-service courses.

What does this book offer?

While there is an increasing number of resources on the background to some of today's controversial issues and guidance on effective pedagogy, this book brings together for the first time the thoughts of people from around the world who are experienced in teaching about such issues. They illustrate that young people need knowledge and understanding of controversies, as well as effective strategies to debate and seek resolution of conflicting positions in order to avoid deadlock and frustration.

The book is in three parts. In the first section, which addresses the controversy inherent in policy decisions, Paul Carr challenges our thinking about the power dimensions which govern educational policy making. His data come from his work in Canada, but is relevant elsewhere. He draws attention to the lack of accountability or transparency in decision making, policies, funding, resources and activities, and unsatisfactory outcomes with respect to social justice. He argues that this is because of the unacknowledged power and privilege of 'whiteness' and the ways in which white people can define the agenda to support their own position, leading to marginalisation of minority groups and contributing to continuing racism in society.

Part Two, Teaching Controversial Issues through the Curriculum, provides detailed strategies and descriptions of approaches with pupils of different age groups. Goodall addresses the challenge of supporting teachers of children in the early years (ages 3-8) in dealing with issues of war and global conflict. She discusses how teachers might support children who have experienced conflict and offers practical advice for teaching all children about war and peace. She draws on peace education and gives examples of co-operative games and conflict resolution activities. Her chapter will be of practical use to many teachers. Working with slightly older primary school children in England, James Hennessy provides a fascinating case study of how to address one of the most troubling controversies of our times – terrorism motivated by strongly held beliefs. Using drama approaches based on a terrorist attempt in the past – the Guy Fawkes rebellion of 1605 – he moves his pupils through experiential activities and reflection to consider present day attitudes and actions.

In a chapter which explores how controversial issues can be addressed through critical reading of fiction and through drama, Myhill points out that critical literacy is an important skill which will help readers appreciate not just the controversial nature of some issues, but that some books are themselves controversial. She focuses upon classroom strategies for working constructively on controversial issues and offers a wide range of practical strategies using drama techniques. She concludes with a list of fiction which can stimulate investigation of contemporary controversies.

Hicks' chapter is about another increasingly topical, urgent and disturbing controversy: climate change. He highlights some of the current debates about sustainable development and problematises the issue, pointing out that there will always be profound differences in the way people view human nature, the goals of life and the means by which these may be achieved. In consequence, there will always be argument about the meanings of sustainability and the best way to respond to climate change, including educational responses. Since our educational and political ideologies determine the way we interpret issues, he challenges teachers to think critically about their approaches in the classroom.

Hughes and Sears' chapter based on work with Russian and Canadian young people draws on controversies in the past – particularly the militant wing of the women's suffrage movement in England – to explore how one might understand different perspectives and consider options. Anne Sliwka's chapter uses contemporary controversies to help students explore options and points of view. She describes an ambitious project in a German secondary school using a technique called 'Democratic Fora'. Large numbers of the school community were involved; students themselves chose the controversy they wished to research and present, for example whether young Muslim women should be able to wear the hijab in the school. *Inter alia*, they heard and questioned the views of members of the legislature, and eventually presented their own positions to an audience of their peers.

The case study from Norio Ikeno addresses a current controversy in Japan which could well be considered by secondary students in other countries: what is the most equitable method of parliamentary representation? Using comparative information from Britain and Germany, the students not only considered the pros and cons of their own system but came to a view on their preferences.

Like Hicks, Versfield's chapter in Part Two deals with a controversial issue related to the environment. Working in the Western Cape, South Africa, Ruth Versfeld asked her secondary school pupils to engage with a major dilemma in the contemporary world – the conflict between environmental needs and the needs of those living in poverty to make a living. Her case study describes in detail how her pupils approached this question – a model which could be used for other controversial issues as the strategies discussed are eminently transferable to other countries and contexts.

Part Three is entitled Whole School Values and Action. It focuses on generic pedagogic issues, including the importance of learning how to participate in democratic procedures, and how to find non-violent ways to resolve conflict.

Alistair Ross concentrates on a neglected area, political education in primary schools. He reviews the research and pedagogy of political educa-tion in the UK and argues that children are capable of dealing with poli-tical issues, and need to address political concepts of power, authority, law and order. He argues that teachers need to move beyond 'safe teaching' about structures and processes and develop a wide conceptual under-standing together with the knowledge and skills to manage participatory debate and democracy in the classroom. His chapter is relevant to those teaching pupils aged 7-14.

Kathy Bickmore's chapter makes the important point that even if we ack-nowledge that there are constructive as well as destructive ways to handle conflict, we need to teach the former, and not assume they are innate. Bickmore describes a variety of practical approaches which have been implemented successfully with pupils of different ages in Canadian schools. She draws on feminist theory and examples and notes that typi-cally female approaches to conflict can enrich democratic resolution of controversy.

The chapter from Fran Martin is on school linking, which is currently be-ing promoted by official bodies and NGOs in Britain. Martin critiques school linking which fails to problematise the relationship between schools, and may perpetuate patronising attitudes. Following a detailed exploration of how linking may reinforce negative prejudices towards the South, she describes a case study where schools have avoided these dif-ficulties and are developing a mutually supportive relationship.

Manju Varma-Joshi draws on her research about the nature and pre-valence of racist abuse suffered by people from minority ethnic back-grounds in a mainly white area of Canada. She highlights the ways in which such communities deny the experience of ethnic minority people and believe that only extreme acts of racism matter. She questions the value of multicultural education and celebrations of diversity to counter racism and offers a number of strategies to challenge racism in the class-room, starting with students' existing knowledge and experience.

Dean and Joldoshalieva draw on their experience of working in Pakistan in their chapter on the challenge of teaching about controversies within an educational climate which has little tradition of encouraging dissenting views. They emphasise the importance of teachers learning strategies for teaching controversial issues so that they can manage the unexpected in the classroom. Like Myhill, they draw on drama techniques, and provide a detailed description of their work with practising teachers at Aga Khan University. The teachers learned about and practised different approaches on their course, and then took the strategies into their classrooms. While the approaches are universal, it is also clear that the overarching issues which concern Pakistani children and their teachers resonate with those which interest young people elsewhere.

The chapters in this book illustrate that teaching controversial issues is not just about knowing your subject matter – though that is important if we are to avoid 'ignorance debating with ignorance'. It is also about the way we approach sensitive issues, the ways in which children are heard, encouraged to talk, challenged and valued. The eleven year olds cited at the beginning of this chapter were asked why they thought they should learn about controversial issues. They replied:

- You learn to argue a point and say why
- We can put ourselves in other people's shoes and see their point of view
- It uses your imagination a bit more
- You're more aware of what's happening in the world
- You get to work together.

The responses show that they valued this work not just because they were better informed about issues which concerned them, but because they valued working co-operatively, arguing their case, thinking creatively and understanding the perspectives of others. We argue that these com-petences are required of today's young people wherever they live, and that creative and sensitive teaching of controversial issues can excite and in-spire as well as prepare children for participation in democratic societies. We are grateful to our authors for sharing their expertise and hope that this book helps put controversial issues back into the heart of education.

References

Arstall, L. (2006) *Scheme of Work for Year 8 – Conflict*, http://www.citized.info/pdf/students/Laura_Arstall_SOW.pdf

Claire, H. (2001) *Not Aliens: Primary School Children and the Citizenship/PSHE Curriculum*. Stoke-on-Trent: Trentham Books

Claire, H. (2003) *Dealing with controversial issues with primary teacher trainees as part of citizenship education*. http://www.citized.info/pdf/commarticles/hilary_claire1.pdf

Claire, H. (ed) (2004) *Teaching Citizenship in Primary Schools*. Exeter: Learning Matters

Davies, I., Gregory, I. and Riley, S. (1999) *Good Citizenship and Educational Provision*. London: Falmer Press

Fiehn, J. (2005) *Agree to Disagree: Citizenship and controversial issues*. London: Learning and Skills Development Agency

Garlake, T. (2003) *The Challenge of Globalisation*. Oxford: Oxfam

Hess, D. (2004) Controversies about controversial issues in the classroom, *PS: Political Science and Politics,* April

Hicks, D. and Holden, C. (1995) *Visions of the Future: why we need to teach for tomorrow*. Stoke-on-Trent: Trentham Books

Holden, C. (2002) Teaching the tricky bits: topical, political and controversial issues, *Education 3-13*, 30 (2), pp17-23

Holden, C., Joldoshalieva, R. and Shamatov, D. (2006) Children as Citizens: an International Perspective. *Paper for the International Conference of Citizenship and Teacher Education*, Oxford: UK

Holden, C. (2007) Young People's Concerns, in D. Hicks and C. Holden (eds) *Teaching the Global Dimension: key principles and effective practice*. London: RoutledgeFalmer

Holden, C. and Hicks, D. (2007) Making Global Connections, *Teaching and Teacher Education*, 23 (1) pp13-23

Oulton, C., Day, V., Dillon, J. and Grace, M. (2004) Controversial issues – teachers' attitudes and practices in the context of citizenship education. *Oxford Review of Education*, 30 (4), pp490-507

Oxfam (2006) *Teaching Controversial Issues: Global Citizenship Guide*. Oxford: Oxfam

Perry, W.G. (1999) *Forms of intellectual and ethical development in the college years: A scheme*. San Francisco: Jossey-Bass Publishers

QCA (1998) *Education for citizenship and the teaching of democracy in schools: Final report of the Advisory Group on Citizenship*, Chair Sir Bernard Crick. London: Qualifications and Curriculum Authority

QCA (Spring 2000) *Guidance: A Summary of Appendix 2 of 'Citizenship at Key Stages 3 and 4*. http://www.qca.org.uk/printable.

Revell, P. (2005) Professionals or parrots? *Education Guardian*, March 8, p2

Richardson, R. (1986) The hidden message of schoolbooks, *Journal of Moral Education,* 15 (1), pp26-42

Robbins, M., Francis, L. and Elliott, E. (2003) Attitudes towards education for global citizenship among trainee teachers, *Research in Education*, 69, pp93-98

Stradling, R., Noctor M. and Baines, M. (1984) *Teaching Controversial Issues*. London: Arnold

Wegerif, R. (2003) Reason and Creativity in Classroom Dialogues, *Language and Education*, 19 (3), pp223-237

Wellington, J. (ed) (1986) *Controversial Issues in the Curriculum*. Oxford: Blackwell

Wilkins, C. (2001) Student teachers and attitudes towards 'race': the role of citizenship education in addressing racism through the curriculum, *Westminster Studies in Education* 24 (1) pp7-21

Educational policy and the social justice dilemma

Paul Carr

In this chapter Paul Carr reveals a controversy at the heart of Canadian educational policy making. The unacknowledged power and privilege of 'whiteness' and the ways in which white people can define the agenda to support their own power, leads to marginalisation of minority groups and contributes to continuing racism in society. He critiques the complacency of public education in its attempts to inculcate social justice and democratic values in the absence of proper accountability and transparency. While these are recognised components of the educational reform agenda, there is nothing equivalent for social justice at the institutional level. The result is lack of accountability or transparency in decision making, policies, funding, resources and activities, and unsatisfactory outcomes with respect to social justice.

Introduction

Who determines what is a controversial issue, and how do we deal with such issues? Such questions, rightly the focus of this book, are themselves controversial. This chapter focuses on how controversial issues are manufactured, massaged and manipulated before they make it to the formal curriculum and policy level. Before teachers have the mandatory policies, directives, guidelines and course-content with which they are to educate and engage students, there is an entirely different, and problematic, process at play that leads to the conceptualisation and development of educational policy. This process, as mysterious as it is misunderstood, is pivotal in determining the shape and parameters of what takes place in the classroom. A particular concern involves the area of social justice: if the educational policy process has not fully internalised social justice considerations, could the curriculum then be taught in such a way as to address social justice concerns?

How do you teach controversial issues within a political environment pre-occupied with the notion of balance, discounting ideology, stressing the positive, and focusing on academic standards? Opfer (2005:ix) has pointed out that the 'myth of apolitical education is long dead even though there is a trend in the education field toward portraying itself as increasingly neutral and objective'. In my experience, a significant number of student teachers have strong reservations about teaching about and for demo-cracy, for fear of being perceived as biased, or of indoctrinating students into a particular perspective. This raises the question of the critical role played by educational leadership to cultivate, support and act in the area of social justice in education for any tangible gains to be made at the class-room level.

The ample research on differentiated outcomes between racial and ethno-cultural groups requires us to consider how the educational system has failed to live up to its promise of providing a quality and equitable ex-perience for all students. This situation necessitates a review of the formal and informal curriculum, and why, for example, some groups claim that it is too Euro-centric, and even racist. In relation to controversial issues, it is important to understand that not everyone comes to school with or from the same vantage-point, requiring that the pedagogy takes into considera-tion different experiences, cultures and learning styles.

This chapter explores notions of identity and power with relation to educational policy development, and delves into policy structures and processes. The notion of Whiteness (Fine *et al*, 2004; Dei *et al*, 2004), centred on the power and privilege accorded the white race, is significant in deconstructing how educational policy is developed. Does the educa-tional policy process effectively encourage, cultivate and integrate a strong social justice component that can then be translated at the teach-ing level into the tools, resources and pedagogy which would enable students to address important and problematic matters in an appropriate and inclusive way? Underscoring this discussion is the conceptual, philo-sophical and applied notion of accountability. How do governments enforce and hold to account the teaching and learning of social justice in support of school activities and engagement? I conclude with a discussion around what can be done to ensure a more inclusive, sensitised and effective policy development process to provide a framework for educators to 'do' social justice work in education.

What is social justice, and why is it important?

How should social justice be conceptualised in contemporary times? Social justice involves a focus on the human condition, equity and difference, and thence on discrimination and other forms of oppression. Within the educational policy context, social justice is concerned with inclusion, representation, processes, content and outcomes from a critical perspective, seeking to contextualise, frame and promote debate and action around these issues. I use the term 'equity' – although there are some nuanced interpretations – as a complement to social justice. Acknowledging the political nature of education is key to the concept of social justice; allowing for, and promoting the inclusion of marginalised voices is fundamental. Vincent (2003) focuses on identity in her definition of social justice, which necessarily requires an analysis of power and privilege, the role of society in constructing lived experience, and the intersections of the myriad components forming one's identity, which coalesce to (re-) define individual and collective experience.

The process of identifying and institutionalising controversial issues is clearly political, as are all decisions made within and about the education system. It is political in the sense that value-judgments are made about the merits of issues, the people presenting them, and the shape of the process to develop and implement policy. Whiteness is a critical concept because white people, in general, are ignorant or unaware of the power and privilege accorded to their skin colour. Colour blindness in societies that have been built on white racial supremacy must be re-considered at the philosophical, political, economic, social and educational levels (Dei *et al*, 2004).

Social justice, in its broadest sense, is the never-ending quest to strive to address and redress marginalisation, inequity and divisive action. Intention is important but it is also critical to consider effect, especially when deconstructing how, for example, racism manifests itself in a systemic, institutional way. Social justice education, therefore, concerns not only the delivery of curriculum but also the development of policies, curriculum and initiatives, as well as the whole range of activities framing decision making, and the nature of the institutional culture. Social justice is also directly linked to the philosophy and application of democracy and citizenship. How could democracy and citizenship exist without social justice? In effect, what education systems do (content) and how they do it (process) are as important as what is achieved (outcome).

The educational policy development process

What happens when a new government takes control? How, if at all, is social justice conceptualised by governments? How does government shape the agenda, the players, and the infrastructure? How, and especially with whom, does it make direct contact in order to discuss issues and proposals? How do diverse interests get on the agenda? What is the connection between policy development and implementation, and how are teachers involved in the process? Educational policy, although crafted in different ways by different governments in different jurisdictions, ultimately involves a similar dynamic. Some political authority, usually in consultation with teachers and the community, determines what the issues will be, and then sets about developing policy on what will be taught, by whom, and how. The process is undoubtedly complex, involves many factors and stakeholders, but its shape and form are pivotal in relation to the outcome.

Politics and policy are inseparable, and the process employed to make decisions has serious implications for what takes place in the classroom. The link between educational policy implementation and policy development is, therefore, integral to understanding the educational experience of students and educators. A critical appreciation of the role and influence of how power is exercised can lead to a more constructive assessment of how policy needs to be re-shaped. For instance, if teachers feel that they were not consulted on a particular policy or reform, they may delay, alter or even block the full extent of the policy implementation. Plaut and Sharkey (2003:1-2) emphasise the necessity of solidifying the relationship between those developing policy and those charged with the implementation, stressing that 'policymakers, many of whom may never have taught, work as action executives... (and) define problems based in part on public opinion'. Achieving substantive, meaningful influence related to equity over the end-product is almost unattainable when decision-making processes are not inclusive and respectful of social justice considerations. Therefore, to introduce progressive ideas, to garner and sustain support, to ensure effective implementation, and to deter massive upheaval and dissent is critically important for there to be any movement in the area of equity.

Young and Levin (1999) emphasise the importance of ideology and national political tradition in studying educational reform in a comparative setting, thus reinforcing the notion that politics cannot be disconnected from the political decision-making process in education. Ministers or Secretaries of Education, following their party leaders, set the tone and establish policy for the educational sector. Their power is immense when one considers that in addition to the positioning and articulation of polices and resources they have the ability to define the language used in the educational sector. Marshall and Gerstl-Pepin (2005:19) illustrate the manipulation of 'policy talk' through terms like 'world class standards', 'ghetto riots', 'strict accountability', 'welfare cheat', 'national security', 'paperwork' and 'red tape' which can sway emotions connected to issues such as school quality, race, poverty, the national budget, innovation, and equity policy. Such terms can be used to collect, condense, and shape opinions so forcefully that alternative views sound irrelevant and unsound.

The literature often speaks of values and choices that emerge in the policy process, involving trade-offs, negotiation and the quest for what is doable, something that may not necessarily be the optimal priority but palatable, given a range of circumstances. If the Government decides that the word 'racism' is no longer to be used, then the tremendous trickle-down rumble throughout the education system manifests itself in a plethora of non-actions. This is what happened in Ontario. The change of governments, from a left-leaning regime – the New Democratic Party (NDP), 1990-1995 – to a right-leaning government – the Progressive Conservative Party, 1995-2003, exemplifies the radical shift in ideas, policies and resources. The transfer of power in 1995 has been considered a watershed moment in Canadian education (McCaskell, 2005). The NDP had an articulated, rhetorical commitment to the equity agenda, with visible policies, programmes and resources. Cabinet-level committees were established on antiracism, making equity a mandatory component of cabinet submissions. This meant that there would be environmental scans, research, studies, consultation and community input into the policy process, which would take into account the concerns and needs of racial minorities.

In effect, the Conservatives abolished the word 'racism' from the educational vernacular during their nine-year mandate. If these matters are not even considered during the policy development process, what chance is there that there will be a solid social justice foundation in the resultant policy? This is not to infer that no work whatsoever would be undertaken in the area of racism but rather to underscore that this area would not be the established, formal priority of school boards, principals and teachers, that it would not figure as prominently in boards' business and strategic plans, and that funding, training, resource documents and policies would not be viewed as fundamental to the institutional mission.

Contributing factors to the education policy process
Resisting change and rupturing progressive work
Introducing social justice-based change requires a sustained effort, focused on working with all sectors to ensure that marginalised groups are not further disadvantaged, and also that all people, regardless of racial or geographic origins, understand the importance of the initiative. Too many simultaneous, competing initiatives, or not enough visible direct support, can lead to rejection of a policy. If teachers are not considered key players in the development and implementation process, the end result will most likely be unsuccessful, since many of the political advisors, as opposed to permanent public servants, come from the political arena and usually have limited educational experience. This is because the way policy is developed (the process) is almost as important as what is achieved (outcome).

Shaping the policy message
The media play a pivotal role in defining the mandate of a government. Hernan and Chomsky (2002) provide an arsenal of analysis on the role of what they call 'coercive and obedient media' in 'manufacturing consent'. Governments spend untold funds on advertising, polling and strategic advice. This is public money, often used to convince the public of the worthiness of a political party's viewpoint, quite separate from the government representing the interests of the people. The question of who is in the media, who controls it, who has access to it, and what images, articles, themes and concepts are most predominant, as well as the emphasis accorded to specific issues, is particularly germane in evaluating the presence and status of social justice within a government's mandate. The issue of bias, misrepresentation and omission in relation to racial minorities in the media is well known. What generally drives the government agenda is not the latest scientific research, nor the *bone fide* needs of the students; political agendas are generally painstakingly crafted to weed out dissenting, and minority, voices.

Controlling the agenda

Once in government, the human and financial resources available to control public debate are almost limitless. Layers of experienced, professional staff – known as public servants or bureaucrats – are dedicated to carrying out the mandate of the government of the day, but are not generally invited to critique the direction of government policy. Increasingly, they are considered the implementers of policy, distanced from the development of policy, which, in Canada, is often the exclusive domain of unelected officials. To suggest proposals that diverge from the official business plan is not encouraged, and those consulted are positioned to build the case in favour of the government platform, which, almost systemically, does not include equity-seeking groups and interests. The expression in Canada that 'the report is gathering dust' is a well-known reminder of the waste of public funds expended on research that uncovers incompatible policy directions. In sum, access to government is pivotal in order to be able to have input into the decision making process.

Developing curriculum and educational policy

There is a conceptual and ideological basis to the drafting of documents, policies and activities which serves as a concrete platform for interaction between teachers and students. What to teach, how, when and to whom, combined with the issue of the process and results, is critical for democracy to flourish. Westheimer (2006:5) questions the orientation of civic education in the United States post 9/11, where he underscores that 'dissent, rather than being an essential component of democratic deliberation, is seen as a threat to patriotism'. In this view 'politics' is something unseemly and best left to mud-slinging candidates for public office: being political is tantamount to devaluing the public good for personal or party gains.' Indeed, service-learning is political, and charity tends to be the most politically acceptable form of involving students in the community, as opposed to social justice work. With an increasingly ethnically diverse population, students clearly need exposure to, and experience with, genuine diversity and social justice. If the policy development process does not cater to the needs and concerns of teachers and students in providing the resources, tools, structure and support, then the effectiveness of the actual curriculum and related service learning may be limited.

White complicity and privilege

Rezai-Rashti (2003) speaks of the commitment of 'equity workers', those who are personally and professionally engaged in the social justice agenda, as exemplified by those on the Toronto Board of Education in the 1980s and 1990s who sought to bring about progressive change from within. Although governments often attempt to appropriate social justice causes, it is extremely difficult to survive as an 'equity worker', constantly challenging the institutional power while at the same time representing the formal government party-line to those demanding change on the outside. Social justice must not be considered uniquely the responsibility of equity workers and advocates; it is a matter of societal interest and importance. Those with decision-making power as well as others who may have some influence also need to be part of promoting social justice. They need to reconcile their own involvement in the way power is shaped, and also consider the true extent of the institutional framework that has predominantly benefited whites.

Building an accountability framework

There is an important distinction to be made between how educational systems actually function, and how they ought to function. One might ask if the system is intended to function for social justice, progressive change and democracy. If inequitable power relations are not fully acknowledged, how can there be anything but the maintenance of the system, the reproduction of social relations and knowledge? Disenfranchised individuals and groups deserve a more equitable, responsive and culturally-sensitive learning experience. Governments enacting legislation and policy intended to better society should be held to account for social justice, in addition to high academic standards. Sunderman (2006) argues that the accountability requirements of the *No Child Left Behind Act* have the practical effect of further marginalising lower socio-economic groups as well as racially diverse schools.

Accountability hinges, in large part, on leadership. As Fullan (2005) suggests, it is critical to develop targets and measures in order to strategically position and advance an educational system. It is imperative that leaders understand and are capable of connecting and working with social justice. Accountability will not be meaningful if education leaders cannot immerse themselves in the institutional culture of their school-systems in such a way as to reverse passive resistance and intransigent behaviours and processes that do not facilitate transformation.

How can educators and stakeholders ensure that there will be a greater level of accountability in education in relation to social justice? A number of areas can be probed by stakeholders – including parents, students, community groups, educators, and others – to seek some documented, demonstrable connections between the rhetoric of accountability and the reality of a progressive, well-rounded education, premised on the notion of political literacy and social justice. In particular, stakeholders should demand that governments provide reports, plans, targets, standards and funding for the following, with a specific focus on social justice: strategic policy and leadership; policy development and decision making processes; inclusion and representation; curriculum, including extra-curricular and service-learning components; community involvement; training; communications; funding; data-collection and analysis; and accountability mechanisms including evaluation, monitoring and review.

Social justice could become the organising principal in planning and developing measures, targets and standards, in support of how resources are allocated and policies evaluated at school, school board and Ministry of Education levels. Progress can be made in achieving accountability if the same rigour, discipline, intensity and resources are consecrated for social justice aims as are dedicated to raising educational standards. Educational systems can make progress if they establish goals and measures for literacy; the same could be done for social justice, with obvious benefits for the entire education system. The conceptualisation and implementation of such an accountability system need not be bogged down in complex institutional manoeuvrings; committed, strategic action on a sustained basis can have a positive effect on improving educational opportunities, processes and outcomes.

A First Nations proverb states that one should 'never judge a person until you have walked two moons in their moccasins'. The privilege to discuss what you wish, and how, is enormous. This basic premise of inequitable power relations has not generally been the focus in the field of educational policy development. The term Whiteness is virtually unknown in mainstream education circles, and, as suggested in this chapter, most white people have the privilege of negating white complicity in racism. It is not just that people find it acceptable, for example, that three times the number of black compared with white youths drop out in the Toronto Board of Education (Ontario, Royal Commission on Learning, 2005). More distressingly, it is rather that questions about why this happens are not even asked at the educational policy level. This illustrates how white power, assumptions and privilege operate. Thompson (2003) frames the issue in terms of accepting the concreteness of white involvement, and getting past the notion that a good effort necessarily means that racism is non-existent. We need to question the way that deficit thinking is produced and reproduced, and the impact that this has in reinforcing assimilation into the dominant culture. Do those who are developing policy strive to address social justice concerns in a manner that facilitates constructive and meaningful engagement in democracy? Outside of the formal written policies and curriculum, how does the educational institutional culture respond to, and support, the diverse needs of a multicultural society?

The power of language has been used to convince broad sectors of society of the high level of democracy and accountability in education. Arguably there is *de facto* democratic racism at play since all of the key forces – including the courts, the legislature, big business, and the media – have virtually achieved consensus that racism is not what people of colour say it is. Right-wing politicians in the United States have invoked the name of Martin Luther King to eliminate affirmative action programs, bastardising the legacy of the civil rights leader. Similarly, in-depth examination of white supremacist discourse indicates that elements of extremist thoughts, concepts and ideology can be commonly found in mainstream organisations and government.

Conclusion

This chapter has argued that some form of a social justice framework at the institutional level is necessary because of the clear lack of accountability for decision making, policies, funding, resources, activities and outcomes. The notion that public education is currently striving to inculcate social justice and democratic values must also be critically examined. Whereas accountability and transparency have become essential components of the educational reform agenda for the past decade for a host of indicators, no such comprehensive set of standards, guidelines and measures exists in relation to social justice education. For there to be a vibrant, fruitful social justice program in education, it would be necessary to acknowledge and reconcile the multi-faceted problematic of Whiteness as it is engaged in, and forms a major part of, racism and marginalisation in society. Connecting the educational policy process with what takes place in the classroom is key to increasing the quality of the educational experience. Effectively dealing with controversial issues in the classroom, with the hope of enhancing political literacy, requires de-constructing the controversy behind the conceptualisation of the educational policy content, which ultimately filters down through lesson plans, textbooks, teaching approaches, school culture and the public mindset toward education.

References

Dei, G., Karumanchery, L. and Karumanchery-Luik, N. (2004) *Playing the Race Card: Exposing White Power and Privilege.* New York: Peter Lang

Fine, M., Weis, L., Powell Pruitt, L. and Burns, A. (2004) *Off White: Readings on Power, Privilege, and Resistance.* New York: Routledge

Fullan, M. (2005) *Leadership and Sustainability: System Thinkers in Action.* Thousand Oaks, California: Corwin Press

Herman, E. and Chomsky, N. (2002) *Manufacturing Consent: The Political Economy of the Mass Media.* New York: Pantheon Books

Marshall, C. and Gerstl-Pepin, C. (2005) *Re-Framing Educational Politics for Social Justice.* New York: Pearson Education

McCaskell, T. (2005) *Race to Equity: Disrupting Educational Inequality,* Toronto: Between the Lines

Ontario Royal Commission on Learning (2005) *For the Love of Learning.* Toronto: Queen's Printer for Ontario

Opfer, D. (2005) Foreword. In Marshall, C. and Gerstl-Pepin, C. (eds) *Re-Framing Educational Politics for Social Justice.* New York: Pearson Education

Plaut, S. and Sharkey, N. (2003) *Education Policy and Practice: Bridging the Divide.* Cambridge: Harvard Educational Review

Rezai-Rashti, G. (2003) Educational Policy Reform and its Impact on Equity Work in Ontario – Global Challenges and Local Possibilities. *Education Policy Analysis Archives,* 11(51), pp1-15

Sunderman, K. (2006) *The Unraveling of No Child Left Behind: How Negotiated Changes Transform the Law.* Cambridge: The Civil Rights Project at Harvard University

Thompson, A. (2003) Tiffany, Friend of People of Color: White investments in Anti-racism, *Qualitative Studies in Education,* 16 (1), pp7-29

Vincent, C. (2003) *Social Justice, Education and Identity.* New York: RoutledgeFalmer

Westheimer, J. (2006) Politics and Patriotism in Education. *Phi Delta Kappa,* 87 (8), pp 608-620

Young, J. and Levin, B. (1999) The Origins of Educational Reform: A Comparative Perspective, *Canadian Journal of Educational Administration and Policy,* 12, pp1-16

Part 2 – Teaching controversial issues through the curriculum

War and peace with young children
Olwen Goodall

Olwen Goodall is an educational psychologist, Early Years teacher and teacher educator. As she points out, the question is not whether we address children's knowledge and experience of conflict, but how we do so. First she explores some strategies for working with refugees and asylum seekers. Then she discusses the importance of peace education for all children, offering a variety of practical strategies to defuse children's anxieties and teach them to collaborate and deal with conflict.

I saw two five-year old boys drawing the Twin Towers, with people jumping off them. They were making plane crashing noises as they were drawing. The Teaching Assistant came up to them and got very cross. She told them off for being disrespectful to the people who had died and their families, and sent them off to do something else.

The children came up to me and said 'Did you see what had happened and how many died?' but the teacher wouldn't discuss it. She just said 'We've got to do Numeracy now.' I think they should have had a moment just to discuss it briefly, and to try to understand it in their own way before going off to Numeracy.

Both these incidents were reported by trainee teachers in England, working in classrooms with four and five-year old children just after the 9/11 terrorist attacks on New York.

However much we might want to shield young children from the scary realities of life at home and abroad, we do not always have the choice. They will have encountered images and stories of horror and violence from the television, radio, newspapers, adults, other children and, sometimes, their own lives. As their teachers it is our role to mediate these images and stories, rather than deny the reality. Such stark global issues fall outside the confines of the safe curriculum usually thought appropriate for young children, and teaching about them is considered controversial. However, I would argue that we are disadvantaging children by denying them opportunities to deal with these topics both rationally and emotionally.

This chapter considers ways to teach children aged three to seven about such issues. It includes teaching children who have themselves been involved in conflict as well as teaching about war and peace as part of the everyday curriculum for all children.

Teaching young children who have experienced conflict

Teachers in the UK may have children from war-torn countries in their classrooms. What issues should these teachers be aware of in order to teach these children most effectively and to integrate them into their classrooms?

A useful starting point is Save the Children's educational resource (2003) for working with refugee children. It has a focus on active learning and suggests ways of providing safety and security in the classroom. The curriculum can incorporate Peace Education which helps teachers to challenge ways of thinking that may prolong conflict and deny human rights.

In addition to the traumas they may have experienced in their countries of origin, refugee children may suffer discrimination and hostility from other children. They may well show generalised stress responses to the cumulative trauma they have experienced. Teachers should look out for signs of fear, anxiety, depression, anger and hostility, self destructive behaviour, feelings of isolation or stigma, poor self esteem, difficulty in trusting others, relationship problems, acting out, problems with concentration and academic performance. The most severely damaged children may show Post Traumatic Stress Disorder. The risk factors for this are: severity of the traumatic event; parental support/distress after the event; temporal proximity to the event; interpersonal trauma (rape or assault); total number of traumas experienced and being a girl (Cohen, 1998).

Teachers need understanding, sensitivity and careful and intelligent observation. But more specific approaches, for example, developing an intake strategy using art and design and providing opportunities for coping through play are also helpful.

Intake strategy
- Learn the child's name and teach it to the class (eg Qadr)
- Remind the class about how to welcome a new person
- Quickly find out what Qadr is skilled at
- Provide a buddy for Qadr and make sure Qadr knows where to sit
- Use visual timetables – the structure will help them make sense of what is probably a very different school day from their previous experience
- Check you have sorted practical details such as dinner money, uniform, and special dietary requirements
- With your class, find out what you can about where Qadr has come from – look it up on a globe, hear his home language, find pictures and music from his home country, talk about why Qadr had to leave and what he has had to leave behind.

Life will still be stressful for Qadr, but these strategies may help smooth some of the roughest edges.

Understanding the child's responses and needs
Young children may manifest their anxieties and the effects of trauma through their play. Refugee children may show some or all of the following in their play:

- a preoccupation with war and violence
- an identification with the oppressor: a child may re-enact war, taking the role of the oppressor, perhaps being violent to other children
- aggressiveness in play
- rigid or emotionless play, inability to elaborate on their experiences, or simply an inability to play
- characteristic drawings, showing violence or featuring very small children

(QCA 2006a:1)

QCA recommend that traumatised children be given space, time, privacy when they need it, favourable attitudes and appropriate materials to play with. Teaching them with care can help them settle into their new school, and act therapeutically to help them regain confidence, self esteem, and trust in adults and peers. Initially, the safest and most healing processes might come through sensory and exploratory play with water, sand, play-doh, cornflour and a range of differently textured objects or sound making items in a treasure box. Extra support is best given by a key worker with whom they can build a close and trusting relationship. Later, small world play, role play and socio-dramatic play can provide opportunities for them to replicate the real world and represent events in their own lives. Stories and books can help here too – some should reflect the cultural background of the children, as should some of the play resources such as dressing up clothes.

Schools may need to work with parents – with interpreters where necessary – to help explain the role of play in their child's development and recovery. They may come from cultures that have different views about the role of school, and not understand the value of play.

Art and design helps newly arrived children to settle, as it is minimally dependent on language and allows opportunities for expression of emotions. Some children may have had few opportunities to experiment with different media, materials and processes and may need sensory play and exploration time before they embark on directed activities.

Teachers should think about:

- alternative tasks to overcome any difficulties arising from specific religious beliefs relating to ideas and experiences the children are to represent (e.g. patterns rather than portraiture for Muslim children).
- access to stimuli, participation in everyday events and explorations, materials, word descriptions and other resources, to compensate for a lack of specific first hand experiences and to allow them to explore an idea or theme

(QCA, 2006b)

Examples of art and design from the child's home country can provide information for the other children in the class in context, so that the country is not viewed as exotic or unusual. Art activities can also be a good opportunity for buddying, where the 'buddy' works collaboratively with the new child or demonstrates the use of new equipment or materials.

Persona dolls are helpful in dealing with issues raised by asylum seekers or refugees. They can be used to discuss fairness, racism and equality with young children in a non-threatening, playful and enjoyable way that is developmentally appropriate (Brown, 2001). Brown advises that the dolls be kept in a special place in the classroom, and only handled by the children during specific sessions. Each doll is given a consistent persona by the teacher – name, character, family, history, lifestyle, likes and dislikes, hopes and experiences. Persona dolls are used to help children think about people's feelings, and to challenge discrimination based on ignorance or lack of experience (Bowles, 2004; Brown, 2001). They are extremely useful for dealing with potentially controversial issues with young children. Training on how to use Persona Dolls is available.

www.blss.portsmouth.sch.uk

School ethos

The ethos of the school is an important factor in the successful integration of refugee children. Rutter (2006) describes research with older children in the UK indicating that about 20 per cent were sympathetic towards asylum seekers and refugees, about 40 per cent uncommitted and 40 per cent hostile. She found that schools provided few opportunities for ethically based discourses on asylum – for example consideration of justice and fairness, or whether the treatment of asylum seekers was right or wrong. Such opportunities can be embedded in classrooms for younger children, by, for example, the use of Persona dolls, Crucially, however, a consistently implemented policy of non-toleration of violence, bullying and taunting is the most important determinant of how well asylum seeking and refugee children are accepted in schools

Teaching young children about war and peace

Teachers need a complex and multi faceted approach when working with children who have experienced war, and children with no direct experience but who struggle to deal with conflicts they see on television. The facts need to be honestly portrayed, alternatives to war considered in the context of looking at both sides and the emotions generated acknowledged and understood.

Teachers should not shy away from addressing the content of the children's play, even if concerned about the children getting upset. They should answer the children's questions honestly and in as much detail as appropriate for their developmental stage without being threatening. Teachers should not insist that children participate in a discussion – some may just want to listen, and others may want to avoid the entire subject. But there should be a safe time for children to express their views and fears, though this can throw up uncomfortable issues at times, including the racist views some children have (Davies *et al*, 2005).

For example, after events like the Asian tsunami or during the war in Iraq, teachers could respond by maintaining a classroom ethos of safety and support, remaining sensitive to children acting out through play, providing relevant Circle Time activities (e.g. Reach for the Stars – described at the end of this chapter), being aware of children's feelings and allowing

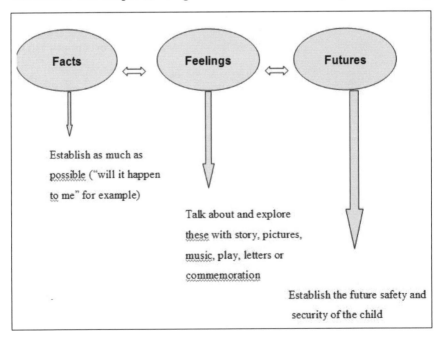

them to express these. Ongoing links with schools abroad can inspire and support children. Dorton Special School for visually impaired children, for instance, has links with Sierra Leone, and regularly involves children from both countries in frank discussions about conflict resolution, drawing on the Sierra Leone children's experiences of war (*TES*, 2005).

When unexpectedly confronted with the kinds of critical incidents mentioned above, teachers have found the framework opposite useful. It provides a sequential structure and the process allows children to feel supported by close and concerned adults, who show that they are affected but not overwhelmed by the incident.

Peace Education

As well as addressing young children's specific fears and questions about local and global conflict, it is important that we educate for peace. Such teaching is for all children – not just for those children living in war free areas. It forms an intrinsic part of the curriculum for many children who come from traumatised and terror ridden areas: Sudan, Somalia, Romania, Northern Ireland, for example. It is a hopeful and serious attempt to foster in young people the attitudes that might help the world change for the better.

Peace can be thought of as more than the absence of violence, injustice and oppression. It is also a belief in non-violence, justice and morality and a sense of partnership and harmony with nature. In Northern Ireland, for example, explicit peace education programmes have been developed to help circumvent some of the worst aspects of the Troubles for young children e.g. 'Getting to Know Me!' for Year 1 and 'The Zig Zag Carpet' for Year 2 (Hall, 1999a, b). 'Let's Talk – Dealing with Conflict in the Primary School' is the final part of this programme for 4-8 year olds (Hall, 2003). It provides children with a simple strategy for dealing with conflict in the classroom; it encourages listening, taking responsibility, looking for solutions and coming to an agreement.

> Education for Peace can carry connotations of political indoctrination, so teachers will need to be aware that they should maintain a balanced viewpoint in the facts and opinions they express, and also be conscious of the role that they take – will they give their own opinion or remain neutral? (Harwood, 1997)

David Hicks has developed a helpful structure to plan a curriculum for Peace Education:

Education for Peace: Outline of a Curriculum

Skills	Attitudes	Knowledge
Critical thinking	Self respect	Conflict
Co-operation	Respect for others	Peace
Empathy	Ecological concern	War
Assertiveness	Open-mindedness	Nuclear issues
Conflict resolution	Vision	Justice
Political literacy	Commitment to justice	Power
		Gender
		Race
		Environment
		Futures

Table 1 (adapted from Hicks, 1988)

Most of the content in the Knowledge column is more suitable for older children, but teachers of young children will recognise much of what is listed under Skills and Attitudes as the focus of many Circle Time activities. Co-operation, empathy, self respect and respect for others, and conflict resolution are key themes in any personal and social education for young children.

The following activities focus on co-operation and conflict resolution and are specifically designed to help children develop their critical thinking skills and extend their emotional vocabulary. Children who can co-operate and resolve conflict among themselves are in a much better position to understand conflict in the world around them. There are also opportunities for teachers to make the link between conflict and co-operation in the classroom and in the wider world.

With all these activities, it is important to allow time for debriefing. Why did that work well/badly? How did it make you feel? How do you think X, Y, Z felt? How could we do it differently next time?

Co-operation games

Many games and activities will allow exploration of several relevant issues – for example discussions about empathy.

- *All aboard*: Talk about what a train does. How do you get on a train? Ask a child to be the train driver. They choo choo around the outside of the circle, then stop behind a child. The driver then says 'All aboard xxxx' and the named passenger gets up and joins the train by holding on to the driver's back. The train continues around the circle choosing another child to pick up. The driver says 'All aboard yyyy' and then the first passenger says the same thing before yyyy can get up and join the train. They all choo-choo round till the teacher calls stop or rattles a tambourine or similar.

- *Count to ten*: the aim is to count to ten as a group randomly, one person calling out 'one', another calling out 'two', another 'three' etc. The catch is that no two children may say a number at the same time. If this happens, everyone starts again. Classes find this very hard as usually about ten children will shout out 'One!' as soon as the signal to start is given. The trick is to use eye contact and learn to wait.

- *Eye contact swaps*: two people establish eye contact across the circle. Without a word, they nod three times and then get up and cross the circle to sit in each other's seats. Only two people can be standing up at any one time. This is an exercise in allowing others to play and being able to wait.

- *Zoom eek*: Identify someone to begin. They turn to the person on their right or left and say 'Zoooom' like a fast car. This starts the car which will now travel around the circle, each child saying 'Zoom' and turning the same way. Once the car has made it all the way round, introduce 'eeek', which should be high pitched. When a child says 'eeek' instead of 'zoom', the car stops and reverses back the other way round the circle, so that the person who has just passed the 'zoom' now says 'zoom' again but passes it back the other way. Sometimes the 'car' gets stuck in one portion of the circle, which can be a useful discussion point and enable development of new rules, like 'boing' which bounces the car across the circle to someone with whom you have made eye contact.

■ *Passing balls*: the children kneel in the circle and the game begins by rolling a ball around the full circle. Every child must touch the ball as it rolls past them. The skill involved is in skimming the ball along with just enough force for it to reach the person next to them and not shoot off across the circle. Once they have established a smooth passage for the ball, introduce another ball into the circle, and another and another. How many balls can we have going at the same time without their catching up or rolling to the middle? This develops concentration and team work skills.

■ *Pass it on*: Practise the song to the tune of London Bridge is Falling Down.

Take the movement, pass it on; pass it on, pass it on, pass it on.

Take the movement pass it on. Can you move like they did?

Model a suitable movement eg waving, standing up, clapping, and explain that as each child takes a turn to go round the circle, they have to copy the movement.

Conflict resolution activities

These too can have several themes incorporated.

■ *Donkeys*: This can only really be done once with each group of children. Two volunteers come up to act as donkeys (they might wear donkey ears). They are lightly tied together (to stop the donkeys straying). They are shown two bowls of sweets on opposite sides of the room, and invariably, a tug of war develops. Before the stronger child can reach the sweets, stop the struggle and ask the class what can be done to solve their problem. Collect suggestions until a child comes up with a co-operative solution; then let the donkeys carry it out and share the sweets around the class. A poster of two donkeys can help to take them through the story again.

An alternative approach is to let the children have the poster first and talk about it, then in friendship pairs stand back to back and hold hands. They have to agree verbally which way to move round the room, taking turns to give instructions, or else they can communicate just by squeezing hands.

■ *Pairs*: The children form pairs. Each pair has a card which has a familiar conflict situation on it. They must think of as many ways as possible to resolve the conflict. For example:

A wants to watch a cartoon on TV. B wants to watch a game show which is on at the same time.

A and B both want the same reading book

At the fair, A wants to go on the roller coaster, but B doesn't. A doesn't want to go on it alone.

This also works well with a group of 4-6. The conflict is presented on a card. The children stick it in the middle of a sheet of sugar paper and brainstorm as many solutions as they can, which one of them, acting as scribe, writes down. The class then comes together to look at all the different solutions to the various problems and talks about which works best.

- *Puppets*: Puppets can be powerfully used with young children to act out similar conflict scenarios to those above, helping them develop alternative responses and solutions.

- *Quarrels*: another Circle Time process uses tag lines – going round the circle and asking each child to complete a starting tag phrase (with the option always of passing if they do not want to participate. They can have another opportunity later if they want.)

'When I saw someone quarrel I felt...' (Make sure they don't identify people by name)

'When I quarrelled with someone I felt...'

'When someone quarreled with me I felt...'

Debriefing can include discussion about what these words mean and where you might use them, and that if they don't like what the person says that doesn't necessarily mean they don't like the person.

These are just a few of thousands of possible activities. The most effective Peace Education will be an outcome of the teacher's sensitive and professional judgment, so as to combine an explicitly planned programme on a variety of themes with responding spontaneously to the multitude of incidents that arise in the classroom.

Futures

We educators must do all we can to ensure that young children are not left in fear of their future and the future of the world. They need opportunities to develop resilience and some sense of control over the future. We know that children from caring and supportive families who have strong friendships best withstand severe psychological stress. These stable and affectionate relationships are one protective factor amongst many others (Cohen, 1998). Save the Children (1996) describes how a large group of unaccompanied boys escaping from the war zone of Sudan had been trained from an early age to adjust and survive in harsh conditions in a nomadic cattle camp away from home. After a harrowing trek on foot to escape through Ethiopia, nearly all showed quick recuperation. Children can be remarkably resilient when they feel supported.

Finally, here's a short activity to help children express their fears, and give them some sense of control over their futures:

- *Reach for the Stars*: You need some cardboard or paper stars, pens, small pieces of paper and a small dustbin or box with a lid.

  The children first write down or draw their fears or worries about the future on small pieces of paper. They screw them up and throw them into the bin, closing the lid resoundingly, and saying something like 'I'm not scared any more'.

  Then, they represent on the stars their vision of what they would like to have happen for the future. A constellation of these wishes can later be created on a Wishes and Hopes Board.

When planning the teaching of controversial issues in the classroom the needs of very young children are seldom considered. This brief account of the numerous ways in which issues of war and global conflict can be embedded in the lives of young children around the world shows that the question is not whether we teach about this, but how. Children know about these horrors – our role is to help them clarify falsehoods and confusions, to help them explore their feelings, and to give them strategies and accurate information so they can think clearly and rationally about conflict and, perhaps more importantly, peace.

References

Bowles, M. (2004) *The Little Book of Persona Dolls*. Leicestershire: Featherstone Education

Brown, B. (2001) *Combating Discrimination: Persona Dolls in Action*. Stoke-on-Trent: Trentham Books

Cohen, J. (1998) Practice Parameters for the Assessment and Treatment of Children and Adolescents with Posttraumatic Stress Disorder, *Journal of the American Academy of Child and Adolescent Psychiatry*, 37 (10), supplement, October 1998

Davies, L., Harber, C. and Yamashita, H. (2005) *Global Citizenship Education: The Needs of Teachers and Learners*. Birmingham: Centre for International Education and Research

Hall, E. (1999a) *Getting to know Me!* Belfast: The Churches' Peace Education Programme

Hall, E. (1999b) *The Zig Zag Carpet.* Belfast: The Churches' Peace Education Programme

Hall, E. (2003) *Let's Talk – Dealing With Conflict in the Primary School.* Belfast: The Churches' Peace Education Programme

Harwood, D. (1997) *Global Express: Tune in to the News.* Manchester: DEP

Hicks, D. (ed) (1988) *Education for peace: Issues, principles and practice in the classroom.* London: Routledge

QCA (2006a) *Play for Asylum Seekers.* http://www.qca.org.uk/10002.html

QCA (2006b) *Primary Art and Design* http://www.qca.org.uk/10075_10589.html

Rutter, J. (2006) *Refugee Children in the UK.* Buckingham: Open University Press

Save The Children Alliance, (1996) *Promoting psychosocial well-being among children affected by armed conflict and displacement: Principles and approaches.* London: International Save the Children Alliance

Save the Children (2003) *Education in Emergencies Toolkit.* London: Save the Children Alliance

TES (2005) Letters from the Front Line, *Times Educational Supplement,* November 25

Children's Books

HEC (2000) *Play on the Line: all children have the right to play.* (Big Book) London: Humanities Education Centre

Heide, F.P. and Gilliland, H.G. (1997) *The Day of Ahmed's Secret.* London: Puffin

Heide, F.P. and Gilliland, H.G. (1992) *Sami and the Time of the Troubles.* London: Clarion Books

Hoffman, M. and Littlewood, K. (2002) *The Colour of Home.* London: Frances Lincoln

Rosen, M. (1996) *This is Our House.* London: Walker Books

UNICEF (2002) *For Every Child: The Rights of the Child in Words and Pictures.* London: Red Fox Books

Walsh, M. (2004) *My World, Your World.* London: Random House Children's Books

Resources for hope: engaging with controversial issues through drama

James Hennessy

James Hennessy's chapter goes to the heart of perhaps the most controversial contemporary issue in society – terrorism. He describes work with
primary aged children as they approach the issues of terrorism and ideological commitment, via a drama set in the early seventeenth century.
Using the Guy Fawkes plot to blow up the Houses of Parliament and
assassinate the English King, he carefully guides children into contemporary and analogous issues.

Introduction

The idea of children actively participating in their own education
continues to be central to drama education. This same idea is also
fundamental to the underlying ethos of citizenship education, and
throughout this chapter this shared aspiration will, I hope, be seen as
more than mere coincidence.

For many people the word 'drama' is associated with entertainment, a play
seen in a theatre, a film on TV or the cinema. This is drama's public face, a
shared experience in a designated space between two groups of people,
where one group performs, usually some kind of story, for another group
of people who passively watch and listen. There is, however, another side
to drama, more concerned with participation, which has benefited from
the work of drama and theatre-in-education practitioners over the years,
making it an unique teaching method. (For a concise history see Bolton,

1998.) In educational settings, a 'process drama' (O'Neill, 1995; Taylor and Warner, 2006) has the potential to create imagined fictional contexts. Working collaboratively, participants are encouraged to take part without any imperative to perform.

Process drama is a powerful tool for learning because it can transform the largely invisible assumptions of our day to day lives and turn them into shared dramatic symbols and metaphors. Active participation can link with the constructs and values of the society and culture we live in, and reveal fresh understandings about our world. Most importantly, the experience has the potential to create a safe but challenging environment in which participants can explore issues which can be very difficult, indeed controversial, in ordinary social or group situations. This is why process drama is so relevant and has such potential in teaching controversial issues.

The example that follows is designed to illustrate this potential. Its content relates to the citizenship curriculum but also stands alone as an authentic experience of drama as education. It is assumed throughout that the children and their class teacher have had some experience of making drama together. The drama was designed for Key Stage 2 (age 9-10). It took place in a school hall – a large space – with the class teacher present, as well as me.

Conspirators

On 7 July 2005, four young men detonated plastic explosives at various points on London's public transport system killing themselves and 52 others. Besides the obvious connection with the attacks on the USA on 11 September 2001, other grim events were remembered: the bombings in Bali (October 2002), Madrid (March 2004) and more recently in Mumbai, North-Western India (July and September 2006). These events were not universally condemned. The perpetrators, labelled 'fundamentalists' by the victims of the plots, believe that their actions are justified. In the current climate, it is extremely contentious to conduct debate directly about the bombings; the rhetoric of understandable anger has eclipsed the limited opportunity for conciliatory dialogue. The circumstances and issues hurtling around these horrendous events recede behind a veil of outrage and confusion, so that most of us are unable to attend to them.

This is true for the children and young people with whom many of us work. What can be done? How can teachers reach beyond the monochrome impressions of these terrorist acts and enable a more thoughtful consideration of the core question that lies at the heart of the atrocities: Why?

It is possible to do so indirectly, through exploring a similar event 400 years ago. 2005 was the 400th anniversary of another act of 'terrorism' in England, the Gunpowder Plot of November 1605, when an attempt was made to blow up King James I and the House of Lords. It is generally assumed that the purpose was to re-establish the Catholic religion, which had undergone many years of censure and persecution by the Protestant state.

Since then it remains the custom to hold firework displays and bonfire parties throughout Britain, on a municipal scale as well as more modest affairs in back gardens. These events often include the burning of a 'guy', an effigy made of old clothes stuffed with newspapers and rags, representing Guy (Guido) Fawkes who was thought – wrongly – to be the leading conspirator. These events have recently merged somewhat with parties associated with the 'ghost and ghoul' themes of Hallowe'en, the eve of All Hallows Day, which falls a few days earlier.

The following process drama explores some of the issues related to the 21st Century's 'war on terrorism' through the lens of the events surrounding the Gunpowder Plot of 1605. The drama also provides opportunities to explore how desperate situations can lead to people making desperate decisions.

If the experience of drama education is to be meaningful it is important to nurture children's engagement. This can take time because drama works best when everyone actively shares the unfolding story. This is a special kind of collaboration wherein the group is caught up in the events of the story *together.* In fact a process drama in this respect is no different from any other kind of drama, be it in the theatre, on TV or at the cinema. Ideally, what all these have in common is an experience that begins with something, an event or incident, that sharpens our curiosity. This particular drama begins by introducing the class to a poem by Charles Causley (1987) entitled *Why?* It is about a child trying to make sense of the ritual of Guy Fawkes about to be burnt on Bonfire Night, ending with the poignant lines:

> It's only a dummy in an old top-hat.
> Nobody's going to die.

The class reflects on the poem and is introduced to key drama conventions. In small groups, using their own bodies as sculptors might use clay, the children form still images of key phrases or words taken from the poem, such as: *the pointing flames jump high*; and *the whizzbangs flash and fly*. This way of working is useful on a number of levels; it encourages the interaction of ideas but it also lays the foundations for what is to follow.

Now the children turn their attention to the girl in the poem: *What is worrying her?* Still in their small groups, the class share their theories, which could be recorded on a large sheet of paper for everyone to see. The children now learn about the Gunpowder Plot and the role of Guido Fawkes. There are many ways of doing this, and there are a lot of materials available in one form or another. What the drama will depend upon, however, is the famous engraving, *The Gunpowder Plot Conspirators, 1605* (see http://en.wikipedia.org/wiki/Image:Gunpow1.jpg). One method could involve providing each group with a pack of contrasting materials which, in varying detail, are concerned with the event. The task would be for each group, working collaboratively, to offer speculations based on these clues.

Working from a picture – who is the spy, who is the conspirator?

Eventually the whole class concentrates on the engraving and in particular the image of Bates – the only person not wearing a hat! – who is being passed a note by a conspirator, Robert Winter. *Who might Bates be? What might the note be about? Who is it for?* It's established that Thomas Bates was a servant to the leading conspirator, Robert Catesby. The children are told to walk freely around the space. They are encouraged to imagine that the space is in the centre of London in 1605. *Everyone is on their guard. News has been heard that there are some who are walking freely through the streets of London who wish to do the new King harm. There are also spies disguised as ordinary people who are searching for clues that will help capture these people. Walk around the space in a way that won't draw suspicion to yourself. Look around, who might be a conspirator, who the spy?*

Everyone in the class stands quite still with eyes closed: *no peeking!* They are told that the teacher will touch one person on the shoulder – this will be the conspirator – and touch another child on the back – this will be the spy. Neither must reveal their identity. They repeat the walking exercise. *Who is the spy? Who is the conspirator?* After a while the children gather in their groups and quietly share their thoughts about these questions – *they mustn't be overheard!* What raises your suspicions? How can you be certain the conspirator or the spy isn't someone in your group?

The exercise is brought to a close and it is revealed that no one was touched – nobody in the class was a spy or a conspirator. Now the teacher encourages general discussion about the experience: *Did you suspect anyone? Why? What thoughts did you have as you walked around? What did you talk about in your groups? How did you feel when you were told there were no conspirators or spies in the group?* This is an opportunity for the children to consider stereotypes, how far inferences might be justified and the notion of 'false positives' and 'false negatives' (blaming the wrong person; failing to identify the right person).

Now volunteers recreate the part of the 'Conspirators' engraving where Bates is being passed a note by Winter, as a still image. The class forms a circle around the two figures and is asked to think what the order to Bates might have been: a short command, even a single word will do. On a signal, the whole class together speak their commands to Bates out loud. *What did that sound like? Was it a hard or a soft sound? Was it relaxed or urgent?* The purpose of this exercise is to nurture the we're-all-doing-this-together quality about the drama, and help externalise meanings and attitudes within the whole group. The exercise reinforces the idea that *Bates was a servant: whatever he himself felt about the command he had to obey.*

The class has had the experience of associating single words or short phrases with still images, either that of the Gunpowder Plot engraving, or the ones they themselves have created in the drama space. Working alone, each child now creates a still image which is based on the title: 'The servant Bates hides the note he has been given'. The teacher selects two or three examples and these are shared with the whole group, inviting comments and suggestions: *Might anyone have seen him hide the note? Who do you think Bates could have trusted with his secret?* The main purpose here is to re-introduce the sense of danger that was authentic to the unfolding history. This creative tension should bind the group together in preparation for what follows.

The whole class now sits down in a circle. They learn that, according to the records of the time, Thomas Bates was a loyal and faithful servant to Robert Catesby. *Bates would not have been given the note unless he was trusted.*

Teacher-in-role as Bates: *I want to thank you for coming to this meeting. As family members and fellow workers, I know you are loyal to our master Robert Catesby – as indeed am I. But I have grave concerns about the note I have been told to deliver.* 'Bates' explains that he suspects their master is planning something very serious and very violent. *If I deliver this note I will be party to this terrible thing. Not delivering this note will be an act of defiance and that would be terrible too – our master would wish me dead.*

Coming out of role, the teacher places the note at the centre of the circle and encourages discussion about Bates' dilemma. This is an opportunity for the children to consider what the Gunpowder Plot depended upon:

- people prepared to commit horrific acts involving killing people, because they believed the very survival of their families and their religious communities depended upon it – this was how Robert Catesby and many other Catholics saw their world 400 years ago
- other people, perhaps those who were close to Bates, who knew something of these terrible plots but were prepared to hold their tongues, being prepared to keep other people's secrets
- powerful people wanting to remain powerful. The trigger to the tensions between Catholics and Protestants can be traced back to the 1520s, during Henry VIII's reign. The break from the Roman Catholic Church was prompted by the Pope's refusal to allow King Henry's divorce from his first wife Catherine of Aragon. It is arguable that the Gunpowder Plot was the culmination of these tensions, although the fear of Catholics continued beyond this date. This is manifest in the 1701 Act of Settlement which bans Roman Catholics and other non-Protestants (and those born out of wedlock) from succession to the British throne. This law has yet to be repealed.

Conscience Alley

To conclude the drama, one of the class is chosen to take possession of the note in the role of Bates. The other children create two lines facing each other, forming a pathway along which Bates slowly walks. The children voice Bates' thoughts as he passes them struggling with his decision: *Should he deliver the note?* When the pupil arrives at the end of 'conscience alley', they are met by the teacher, who assumes another role:

Bates! I have been watching you for a long time. I am a spy for His Majesty King James and you, I believe, are a conspirator. You have information I need – give me the note.

The decision to hand over the note will depend on the work that has led to this critical point: *Would the servant Bates betray his master Catesby and the other conspirators by handing over the note? Or would he remain loyal and faithful for the sake of the cause?*

The 'Spy' now involves the whole class: *Do you know anything of this note? Have you heard this man* [Bates] *talk of a plot to kill the King?* Again, the response will depend on the overall level of engagement of the children with the drama, and their own sense of loyalty to the character Bates, in particular. According to the chronicles of the time, the conspirators, including Catesby and Bates, believed that drastic action was warranted to end the persecution of Catholics. The children learn of Bates' fate: the Gunpowder Plot failed, or what seems more likely, was betrayed. The conspirators escaped, except Fawkes who was arrested in the cellars below Parliament on the night of 4 November. The others were tracked to Holbeche House in Staffordshire and after a siege, during which Robert Catesby was shot dead, Bates was caught and with the other surviving conspirators, was eventually executed by being hung, drawn and quartered, the customary sentence for traitors at this time.

On 9 November 1605, King James made a speech to Parliament in which he stated,

> For although it cannot be denied, that it was only blind superstition of their errors in religion, that led them to this desperate devise; yet does it not follow, that all professing that Romish religion were guilty of the same ... (http://www.royal.gov.uk/files/pdf/jamesi.pdf, accessed August 2006)

Back in the classroom – connecting with current events

The circumstances surrounding the Gunpowder Plot of 1605 in general, and the imagined experiences of Thomas Bates in particular, provide a powerful learning environment within which to explore recent terrorist events. The principal aim of the post-drama session is to reflect upon the question: *Is there a cause or a belief so important that it warrants violence to defend it?* For the children, Bates is the principal character in the drama who embodies this question, or at least provides the class to return to the earlier question: Why? Why did Bates do what he did? Grappling with this does not condone or support his actions. Neither will it bring the class to a clear and final answer.

What it will do, however, is provide an opportunity to approach our own troubled times through the distancing effect created by exploring another event, long ago. The process drama offers an experience – a learning environment – in which all involved can occupy two worlds at the same time: the world which the *history* of the Gunpowder Plot occupies and the world we live in now. The Brazilian theatre practitioner, Augusto Boal (1979), would describe this as 'the participation of one world in another' – Russian doll-like. It is also how metaphors work; good ones provoke fresh thinking about things we may take for granted.

The drama may also help the children approach a separate but related issue. It is clear from King James' speech (see extract above) that the official view regarded the conspirators' 'errors in religion' as the principal motive for the 'desperate devise' in the cellars of Parliament. The view that 'all professing that Romish religion were guilty of the same ...' resonates particularly strongly with the steady rise of Islamophobia in Britain today. Drawing on the similarities of this alarming trend with the parallel circumstances of 16th and 17th century Britain would provide a useful way to conclude the session.

Conclusion

The rhetoric being used nowadays in connection with those who commit or plot terrorism has a marked similarity to the language used in 'the King's great Council' during James I's reign. This early 17th century monarch and the USA's 21st century president were and are committed to 'ridding the world of evil-doers'. The problem with this kind of rhetoric is not only that it prejudges issues, preventing exploration of the ethics and consequences, but that it may also block our ability to learn from the past.

We live in worrying times. Not least because the idea of 'ridding the world of evil-doers' is an aim that does not really help address our fear of and confusion about the recent terrorist events that have caused so much bloodshed and horror. Working with children using drama in the way described in this chapter presents teachers with many challenges. But it can be a welcome respite from the demands of much of the National Curriculum, which is concerned with finding the correct solution or the right answer. Drama education is much more fuzzy, much more open to interpretations; it's an alternative, controversial, approach – more concerned with the formulation of the right questions and identifying the actual problem than with providing correct solutions or right answers.

References

Boal, A. *(1979) Theatre of the Oppressed.* London: Pluto Press

Bolton, G. (1998) *Acting in Classroom Drama: a critical analysis.* Birmingham: University of Central England/Trentham Books

Causley, C. (1987) 'Why?' in *Jack the Treacle Eater.* Basingstoke: Macmillan

O'Neill, C. (1995) *Drama Worlds: a framework for process drama*, Portsmouth NH: Heinemann

Taylor, P. and Warner, C. (2006) *Structure and spontaneity: the process drama of Cecily O'Neill.* Stoke-on-Trent: Trentham Books

http://en.wikipedia.org/wiki/Image:Gunpow1.jpg – for picture of the Gunpowder plot

http://www.royal.gov.uk/files/pdf/jamesi.pdf – for King James' speech after the Gunpowder Plot was discovered

Reading the world:
using children's literature to explore
controversial issues

Debra Myhill

In this chapter Debra Myhill focuses upon classroom strategies for working constructively with books – particularly fiction – which deal with
controversial issues. She discusses the importance of developing critical
literacy in young readers, distinguishing books about controversial
issues from controversial books where the controversy may lie in being
read through different critical lenses. She offers a wide variety of practical strategies for working with pupils, using drama techniques. She
ends by providing a list of fiction which can stimulate investigation of contemporary controversies.

So I have a new name – refugee.
Strange that a name should take from me
My past, my personality and hope.
Strange refuge this.
So many seem to share this name, refugee,

Yet we share so many differences.
I find no comfort in my new name.
I long to share my past, restore my pride,
To show I too, in time, will offer more
Than I have borrowed.
For now the comfort that I seek
Resides in the old yet new name
I would choose.
Friend.

Ruvimbo Bungwe, aged 14

This chapter opens with the voice of a child. Ruvimbo Bungwe joined a school in London as a refugee from Zimbabwe and was one of a group of children to visit the House of Commons to make presentations to Ruud Lubbers, the United Nations High Commissioner for Refugees. Her words are powerful, written from experience; words which hold out a hand of friendship across different worlds and different lives; words which illuminate how reading can change the way we think, feel and understand. It was Paolo Freire (1987) who coined the phrase, 'reading the word and the world' in his seminal argument that literacy is a necessary pre-requisite for liberation, social consciousness and eventual empowerment. He argued that the ability to read and write enabled democratic participation: being literate helped oppressed and minority groups to work collaboratively against social or political forces which marginalise and segregate. For Freire, the act of reading was not a functional skills-based competence, but an act of critical engagement which helps readers to understand and to question the world in which they live.

Children's literature in the UK, particularly that written for teenagers, has undergone a huge expansion in the past twenty years. Commercially, it has been a publishing boom, creating a whole new genre of teenage literature. But the market growth reflects a changed conceptualisation of the child as a reader, recognising that adolescents need reading material which bridges their childhood reading experiences with the adult ones which hopefully lie ahead. One of the strongest trends in recent years has been the emergence of both the 'issue-based' book and books that have themselves been highly controversial. In part, this has been due to a recognition that books for teenagers do not need to be comfortable and moralistic, with happy endings, but that teenagers can enjoy engaging with complex, controversial and difficult issues.

This chapter focuses upon classroom strategies for working constructively with books which deal with controversial issues. Although it is principally oriented towards secondary English classrooms, many of the approaches suggested are readily adaptable to the upper primary classroom or to cross-curricular secondary contexts, and are especially relevant to citizenship education.

Reading as an active process

Reading is not a mono-focal, one-way activity: it is a complex interaction between reader, text and context. As we read, we bring to the act all our previous reading experiences, our own life experiences, and our cultural knowledge and values. When Freire talked of 'reading the world', he meant not simply that books can open up new worlds and new experiences to readers, but also that when we read we have to understand the context in which the words exist. The context encompasses the world represented by the text, the ideas and stance of the author and the world inhabited by the reader. And as we read, we participate in creative transformations of words to ideas, understandings and imaginative engagement. It is a constructive endeavour of making personal meaning from text, not one of passively absorbing a message coded by the author of the text. Moreover, reading makes use of our social, moral and cultural understanding. Can post-Holocaust readers read *The Merchant of Venice* in the same way as Shakespeare's audience? Can post-feminist audiences laugh at Petruchio's treatment of Kate in *The Taming of the Shrew*?

One important aspect of using texts as a medium for exploring controversial issues is to recognise that texts are artefacts, not embodiments of truth, and that effective readers can interrogate texts critically. Critical literacy is a key consideration in approaching controversial issues because it invites readers to become adept at investigating standpoints, values and choices, which are inherent in all texts. In Australia, children working with teachers on developing a critical approach to reading have devised a student-friendly definition of critical literacy, which is used as a starting-point for questioning texts:

A working definition of critical literacy.

- Any text is made in a particular society at a particular time. This influences the form it takes and the ideas it represents.

- Any text gives you a particular version (or part) of a story: it emphasises certain things; and it has gaps and is silent about certain things.

- Texts don't contain one definite, fixed meaning put there by the author. Different kinds of readers in different societies and times can produce different meanings for the same text because of what they bring to it.

- Any text offers you a way of seeing and valuing things and invites you to accept its version as the truth, the way things are meant to be. What comes to be accepted as the truth, the knowledge, comes to serve someone's interests. (Morgan, 1997)

Morgan is inviting readers to question who wrote the book, why they wrote it, and what values and opinions are embedded in the book. An interesting example of this is Theodore Taylor's *The Cay*. This story, set in the Caribbean, tells of a privileged white boy, Philip, who is shipwrecked by a wartime bomb with his black servant, Timothy, on a deserted island. In the struggle for survival, Philip comes to learn that many of his ideas about Timothy are wrong. It was a popular classroom choice for shared reading because it was viewed by many as an antiracist book: it won the Jane Addams Children's Book Award in 1970, awarded to well-written books which promote equality, peace and social justice.

However, this opinion of the book was predominantly voiced by white readers. The book provoked strong criticism from black groups who argued that the book was, in fact, racist, seen through the eyes of a white boy (and a white author) and that it promoted racist attitudes and stereotypes. Taylor handed back the Jane Addams Award in 1975. A critical literacy approach to this novel would raise all these questions about the values and assumptions of the author and the text.

Books about controversial issues or controversial books?

Theodore Taylor's *The Cay* is a controversial book for the reasons outlined above. In thinking about using children's literature to address controversial issues in citizenship, it is important to recognise that books may be controversial in their own right or may be dealing with a controversial issue. Some books written for teenagers are controversial because of their content: Melvin Burgess's *Doing it*, for example, is a highly explicit portrayal of teenage boys' sexual exploits, with a rich seam of vernacular language. Kevin Brooks' novel *Martyn Pig* tells the story of a how a boy murders his abusive father and how he deals with the difficulty of disposing of the body. Both books have been controversial because of uncertainty about the appropriateness of the content for the targeted teenage audience. It is worth observing that these books are rarely deemed controversial by teenagers themselves but only by adults. Both Burgess and Brooks are very clear that they are writing for teenagers, not for parents or teachers, and they are addressing the things which interest and concern teenagers.

On the other hand, there are other books whose content deals with a controversial issue: for example, black segregation in *Yankee Girl* by Mary Ann Rodman; refugee status in *Refugee Boy* by Benjamin Zephaniah and *The Other Side of Truth* by Beverly Naidoo; apartheid and prejudice in

Malorie Blackman's *Noughts and Crosses*. Books like these, which deal with controversial issues of global significance, are valuable potential resources for developing responses to and understanding of controversial issues. In particular, the combination of imaginative identification with characters in novels, plus the psychological safety that fiction provides makes it a rich resource for dealing with controversial issues: it 'presents a safe way to explore troubling realities and concerns and to address some of the prejudices and assumptions that we may have internalised without even being aware of it' (Stones, 2002).

Using texts in the classroom to address controversial issues

For many English teachers, using text as a starting-point for discussion is the bread-and-butter of the subject, and inviting speculation and exploration of ideas, problems or narrative events in fiction is at the heart of responding to texts. But addressing controversial issues using fiction does require sensitive setting-up and management, particularly in helping children to see and understand alternative perspectives, and in supporting them to negotiate consensus or handle agreeing to differ. For this reason, the classroom strategies I offer in this chapter are either drama strategies or discussion strategies, rather than written activities. Drama and discussion not only provide effective contexts for considering controversial issues but both also provide valuable contexts for learning how to participate in democratic debate.

Using drama to explore controversial issues

Drama has two particular strengths in exploring controversial issues. Firstly, through drama, children take on roles which give them the psychological safety to express ideas and opinions which they might fear to explore if they were taken as their personal opinion. For the teacher, and other participants, it is also easier to challenge or question these ideas, as they are not overtly and personally expressed by an individual child but by a character in role. Secondly, drama enables the exploration and understanding of alternative perspectives and this helps to unpack the essence of the controversy at the heart of a controversial issue.

Conscience Alley

Conscience Alley is a drama technique which exposes conflicts, dilemmas and dichotomies and invites participants to think of multiple perspectives on an issue or a situation. The starting-point should be an event or a dilemma raised by a novel, such as the decision whether to award Alem's father asylum in Benjamin Zephaniah's *Refugee Boy*. One child is chosen as the judge, and the rest of the class forms an alley. Children on one side of the alley tell the judge reasons why asylum should be granted, and those on the other side of the alley give reasons why it should not. The judge walks down the alley, listening to all the arguments and at the end has to come to a decision.

A similar strategy is to use the 'Good Angel, Bad Angel' technique. A participant takes on a character from a novel who has a difficult decision to make, and two other participants take on the role of a good angel and a bad angel who give advice to the character on how they should act.

Thought tracking

This is a reflective technique which interrupts a piece of drama and slows things down to create a reflective space. Groups are asked to create a piece of improvisation, prompted by a book: for example, in Mary Ann Rodman's book *Yankee Girl*, new girl Alice finds herself caught up with her cheerleader friends in the racial harassment of African American classmate, Valerie Taylor. The action is stopped and frozen at a relevant point and either the actors themselves say what they are thinking or the audience is invited to articulate their thoughts and motivation at that point in the drama.

Take the power

Many controversial issues have at their heart power relationships between groups; rich landowners who want to cut down rainforest for farmland; ethnic groups where one has more power than the other; unfair trading relationships between the developing and the developed world and so on. Many novels explore such power relationships, both on an interpersonal and inter-group level. 'Take the power' is a drama technique which explicitly draws out these power relationships but which more significantly, invites participants to think about how the power relationship can be changed. Beginning with a scenario from a novel, such as a family argument about valuing British and Asian cultures from Rukshana Smith's novel *Sumitra's Story*, groups develop a tableau which shows the power relationships at a particular point in the argument. A watching participant has to enter the group: they adopt a character and take up a position in the group which changes the power relationships, taking the power away from the powerful person and giving it to someone else. For example:

Sumitra is having an argument with her father, who is standing over her in a dominant position; her mother enters and stands between Sumitra and her father and looks him in the eye.

Hot-seating

This is such a familiar drama technique yet it is so often badly executed! Typically, hot-seating in practice involves a participant sitting at the front of the class and in a rather embarrassed fashion, giving somewhat brief answers to questions from the class. With proper preparation, however, it can be an excellent way to explore thinking on a controversial issue. It is often best done in groups initially, rather than at the front of the class but if participants become comfortable with the technique, it can shift to a front-of-class situation. Hot-seating is first and foremost a questioning technique and the best hot-seating follows reflective preparation of the questions. With a controversial issue, such as apartheid – albeit black oppression of whites – in Malorie Blackman's *Noughts and Crosses,* it could be further developed by allocating groups a character from the novel where the questioning has to be the kinds of question that character might ask. So Sephy's father might be in the hot-seat, with groups preparing questions from the point of view of Callum, Callum's mother, Sephy and so on.

Mantle of the Expert

This is a drama technique developed by Dorothy Heathcote (1995). Pupils take on roles as experts and explore a fictional situation; the teacher may give them 'expert' information or they may research the information in advance, but the participants assume responsibility for the activity. As Neelands (1990) describes it, 'The group become characters endowed with specialist knowledge that is relevant to the situation ... the situation is usually task-oriented ... power and responsibility move from teacher to group; learners feel respected by having expert status'.

An example of a Mantle of the Expert approach might be to take the conflict in Northern Ireland as represented by Joan Lingard in *Across the Barricades* and to set up an Education Board of Enquiry, with experts from the Catholic and Protestant churches, the Northern Ireland Education Minister, the headteacher of a Belfast Integrated School, and a parent governor from one Catholic and one Protestant school. The Education Board of Enquiry has to discuss segregated schooling in Northern Ireland, the issues of faith schools, and whether Northern Ireland should move to a wholly integrated system.

Generating high level classroom discussion on controversial issues

Discussion is an essential element of addressing controversial issues because potentially it gives every child a voice and, handled effectively, it opens up awareness of the range of views available on a particular topic and is democratic because no-one controls the 'right' answer. However, enabling effective discussion is not easy and requires both careful preparation and a willingness as teacher to accept a different pedagogic role. It is also important to remember that there are often genuinely opposing views in a class and that discussion in which a dominant view is given authority can marginalise minority perspectives. I have watched lessons debating fox-hunting where the teacher has assumed that the class held an anti-hunting stance, not realising the strongly held views of some children from farming backgrounds; likewise, in the period of marches against the Iraq war, I have observed anti-war discussions in classrooms where several children had fathers in the navy.

With many controversial issues, there is frequently what could be described as a 'middle class consensus' which, instead of opening up real debate, can simply endorse and promote one viewpoint. Above all, good discussion is dependent on participants who can listen as actively as they can speak, or else the discussion is reduced to the articulation of a series of already held and unchanged views. As Freire (1997) said 'Only those who listen, speak. Those who do not listen end up merely yelling, barking out the language while imposing their ideas'.

Dialogic debate

Dialogic talk is at the heart of good discussion. Dialogic talk owes its origins to Socrates, who used dialogic talk as a way of teaching his students. It is a dialectical process, whose aim is to promote critical thinking, and in which teacher and student share a joint inquiry in the search for a truth unknown to both parties. It is the *process* which is important: by engaging in genuine dialogue with others, individuals can operate at a higher level of thinking than would be possible on their own. However, generating dialogic talk requires a pedagogic shift from the dominant discourse pattern of the classroom to a more open-ended, exploratory discourse. Skidmore (2002) describes this as a shift from *pedagogic dialogue*, which is teacher-controlled and has closed interaction with limited opportunities for participation, reflection or extended contributions, to dialogic pedagogy, which is teacher-managed interaction in which the dialogue is all-important, where children voice their own evaluative judgements, within an open structure and a participatory mode of interaction.

Pedagogic dialogue	Dialogic pedagogy
Controlled by teacher	Shared control between teachers and pupils
Directed towards right answers	
Right answers are valued	Directed towards exploring possibilities
Closed teacher questioning	'Wrong' answers and risk-taking are valued
Teacher has more 'talk time' than pupils	
Limited participation	Open-ended speculative teacher questioning
Outcome focused	Pupils have more 'talk time' than teachers
Teacher owns the truth	
	Inclusive participation
	Unpredictable
	Truth is the shared outcome

To enable this kind of productive discussion to occur, you need to plan for the discussion and be very confident about the topic or the learning being tackled. In order to avoid narrowing down the dialogue and creating an impression that there is an appropriate, pre-determined conclusion to the discussion, the discussion leader has to be able to listen to children's responses and ask questions at key points which will help to move the debate on. Moreover, to promote genuinely open discussion about controversial issues, a discussion leader has to know the topic well, understanding its multiple perspectives so that they can introduce counter-points or alternative lines of thinking at appropriate points.

The current popularity of dialogic talk is largely due to the work of Robin Alexander (2004), who has written about the value of dialogic talk and has undertaken extensive work in primary schools on developing dialogic ways of working. Alexander summarises the key principles of dialogic talk thus:

Dialogic teaching is:

- *collective: teachers and children address learning tasks together, whether as a group or as a class*

- *reciprocal: teachers and children listen to each other, share ideas and consider alternative viewpoints*

- *supportive: children articulate their ideas freely, without fear of embarrassment over 'wrong' answers; and they help each other to reach common understandings*

- *cumulative: teachers and children build on their own and each others' ideas and chain them into coherent lines of thinking and enquiry*

- *purposeful: teachers plan and steer classroom talk with specific educational goals in view*

(Alexander, 2004)

Buzzing

The temptation to give feedback on children's responses can be overpowering, but this merely confirms to the participants that there is one right answer to the debate, and shifts the focus from shared enquiry to teacher-led talk. One way to foster the comfort of both teacher and pupils with discussion but no feedback is to run a Buzz Session. In a Buzz Session, children have had an opportunity to think about something and summarise their thinking in one or two bullet points or sentences. For example, the class might have been considering in a group activity whether Frikkie in *Waiting for the Rain* is responsible for his actions towards Tengo or whether he is a victim of the system he inhabits. At the end of the activity, each individual writes down what they think, and then the teacher buzzes round the class, taking answers from as many children as possible, and creating a sense of ideas buzzing around the classroom. No response should be given to any of the pupils' contributions and the class should be encouraged to look at each other during the buzz session rather than at the teacher.

Listening Triads

The basic principle of Listening Triads, that two people talk while one listens, can be used in a variety of ways to encourage reflective dialogue. The two people talking could be discussing an issue, such as why, in

Frances Mary Hendry's novel *Chandra*, Chandra's parents don't intervene to protect their daughter. Alternatively one partner could be questioning the other on the topic. The third person in the triad listens to the questioning or discussion, preparing to feed back a summary of the key points of the discussion, but not making a contribution. Feedback to the whole class can allow everyone to hear a summary of the discussion from, say, four triads. Alternatively, and with the right classroom space this works particularly well, the triads could join to form groups of six or nine, to which the listeners in the triads give their feedback so that the rest of the group now listen to the 'listeners'. Providing space for both speaking and listening can be a strong foundation for moving into discussion in groups.

Peer questions and envoying

In conventional classroom discourse, teachers ask questions and children answer them. Generating questions from children, however, gives them ownership of the discussion. Moreover, children tend to select questions which reflect their thinking on the topic, so it is a useful assessment strategy. Having read either the whole novel or reached a particular point in the novel, children generate two or three questions raised for them by the book. The questions have to be open-ended, with no right answer, and they must be questions the group feel they could not answer confidently themselves. Sometimes this is easier if the group generate a lot of questions and then select the three that puzzle them most. The three questions are written clearly on index cards and one person in each group is selected as the envoy. This person takes the questions and moves to another group: that group then discusses their response to the questions while the envoy listens. Finally, the envoys return to their original groups and feed back to the original group what the host group had said in answer to their questions.

Diamond Nine

This is a strategy to develop dialogic talk and speculation in groups rather than a whole class context, but it also forces the need to achieve consensus and negotiate disagreements. In advance, the teacher prepares nine cards with statements on an issue – or on a character's behaviour and motivation – which are as diverse and wide-ranging as possible. In small groups of no more than four or five, the nine cards are read and discussed. The group must arrange them in a diamond shape with the statements they agree with most at the top and those with which they agree least at the bottom, as illustrated overleaf:

The Diamond Nine shape cannot be altered to any other geometric varia-
tion, and this forces decision-making and disagreement! This is an important element of the Diamond Nine strategy: it involves weighing up
arguments, listening to one another, logical thinking and dealing with
dissent. It is a useful precursor to whole class discussion on that topic as it
opens up debate and alerts participants to the range of thinking on the
topic, but it rarely resolves the discussion.

Questioning the author

Questioning the author alters the nature of the task from open-ended enquiry to critical thinking about authors and texts and how every text is an
artefact, something created, and which has a purpose. On completion of
reading a book, and building on the skills of critical literacy, children are
asked to devise a series of questions they would ask the author. These
should not be the rather comfortable and obvious questions but questions
which go beyond the surface, such as:

- What is your own view on this topic?
- Whose views are not represented in this book?
- What choices have you made about what to include and what to
  leave out?
- Why did you describe xxx as yyy?

This should be followed by a discussion of how the book has presented
and represented the controversial issue, and particularly the gaps and
silences in the book and the selection of narrative material to present
ideas or characters in a certain light.

Fictional controversies: classroom conflicts and confrontations

If we actively invite children to read the word and read the world, and if we
encourage open-ended dialogic talk, then we may potentially create classroom situations which require careful handling. On one level, this might

include dealing with over-heated debate or over-aggressive responses to peers, and participants may need explicit support in learning to listen and learning how to disagree without causing offence. On another level, however, using books to address controversial issues can bring unexpected standpoints in the classroom to the surface and create difficult situations. A book is not a monolithic entity that encapsulates a specific meaning. So where the readers' own personal experiences and understandings are very different from the writer's or the teacher's, the meanings made by the reader may be very different from those anticipated by the teacher.

This sometimes arises when reading a book which is overtly trying to challenge racism. Attempting to redress racist attitudes can certainly raise unexpected issues, and it would be naïve to assume that attitudes which are often deeply ingrained will be easy to challenge. We need to remember that what the reader brings to the texts is as important as the text itself; a child with racist views will not be transformed by reading an antiracist text, so the process of reading, interpreting and expressing views needs mediation. Equally, our own attitudes as teachers may cause us problems. If we are committed to an antiracist perspective, it can be hard to handle any offensive viewpoints children express in a way that challenges without preaching.

It is also possible that our own, unrecognised, racist views might affect the way we teach about race equality. Linked to this, we should consider how our own ethnicity influences how we represent alternative ethnic voices. In trying to address racism through children's literature, there are two common pitfalls to avoid. The first is the unintentional promotion of racism by feeding prejudice unwittingly: whether by suggesting that race is a problem, because all the children's encounters with texts are about the negative aspect of being a victim of racial abuse; or by promoting a view that cultural diversity is cultural oddity because texts show the 'strange things' other cultures do. Secondly, there is a danger of suggesting that racism is all about colour: because racism is often constructed as a black/white issue it is easy to give this impression. We need to ensure that we also address things such as antisemitism, or ethnic conflict fed by religious difference such as Northern Ireland or Bosnia. It is often helpful to link racism with other forms of prejudice and bigotry.

Ultimately, using fiction as a medium for exploring controversial issues is about drawing on readers' cognitive and affective responses to texts – it is about both thoughts and feelings, about both logical thinking and empathic identification. Used well, fictional narratives promote three-dimensional ways of thinking and understanding issues which are too often presented two-dimensionally and at their best develop individuals who, in Beverly Naidoo's (1993) words 'can cope with ambiguity, understand alternatives, recognise different perspectives at the same time as feeling committed to the idea of humanity.'

Some recommended fiction for exploring controversial issues

Title	Author	Topic
The Other Side of Truth	Beverley Naidoo	Refugees
Refugee Boy	Benjamin Zephaniah	Refugees and asylum
Sumitra's Story	Rukshana Smith	Asian/British culture clashes
Noughts and Crosses	Malorie Blackman	Apartheid
Waiting for the Rain	Sheila Gordon	Apartheid
Mischling Second Degree	Ilse Gordon	Nazism
Yankee Girl	Mary Ann Rodman	US racial segregation in 1950s
Chandra	Frances Mary Hendry	Status of women in India
Tough Luck	Berlie Doherty	(Racist) bullying
Buddy	Nigel Hinton	Class and race 'differences'
Comfort Herself	Geraldine Kaye	African/British culture clashes
Does my head look big in this?	Randa Abdel-Fattah	Wearing hijab
Dear Nobody	Berlie Doherty	Teenage pregnancy and abortion

Title	Author	Topic
Blue	Sue Mayfield	Teenage suicide
Brother in the Land	Robert Swindells	Nuclear weapons
Across the Barricades	Joan Lingard	Northern Ireland conflict
Postcards from No Man's Land	Aidan Chambers	Sexual orientation
From the Notebooks of Melanin Sun	Jacqueline Woodson	Sexual orientation

References

Alexander, R. (2004) *Towards Dialogic Teaching: rethinking classroom talk.* Cambridge: Dialogos

Freire, P. (ed) (1997) *Mentoring the Mentor: A critical dialogue with Paolo Freire.* New York: Peter Lang

Freire, P. and Macedo, D. (1987) *Literacy: Reading the word and the world.* South Hadley, MA: Bergen and Garvey

Heathcote, D. and Bolton, G. (1995) *Drama for Learning: Dorothy Heathcote's Mantle of the Expert Approach to Education.* Portsmouth, NH: Heinemann

Morgan, W. (1997) *Critical Literacy in the Classroom.* London: Routledge

Naidoo, B. (1993) *Through Whose Eyes?* Stoke-on-Trent: Trentham Books

Neelands, J. (1990) *Structuring Drama Work.* Cambridge: Cambridge University Press

Skidmore, D. (2002) From Pedagogical Dialogue to Dialogic Pedagogy. *Language and Education,* 14 (4), pp283-296

Stones, R. (ed) (1999) *A Multicultural Guide to Children's Book 0-16+,* London: Books for Keeps

Ruvimbo Bungwe poem: http://hardy.amnesty.org.uk/images/ul/N/NUT_article.pdf

Education for sustainability: how should we deal with climate change?

David Hicks

In this chapter, David Hicks looks at education for sustainable develop-ment as a controversial issue, examining its origins and the ideological debates surrounding it. Focusing on climate change, he explores why this is a controversial issue, pointing out that our beliefs about its impor-tance are not just about evidence but also about different world views, including ideological and political differences. There will always be pro-found differences in the way people view human nature, the appropriate goals of life and the means by which these may be achieved, he argues. In consequence there will always be debate about the meanings of sus-tainability and the best way to respond to climate change and how education should address the issue.

The context

The UN Decade of Education for Sustainable Development began in 2005, marking international recognition of the need for education to address issues of sustainability (http://portal.unsco.org/education). In the English national curriculum this is taken to be a cross-curricular concern.

> Education for sustainable development enables pupils to develop the knowledge, skills, understanding and values to participate in decisions about the way we do things individually and collectively, both locally and globally, that will improve the quality of life now without damaging the planet for the future. There are opportunities for pupils to develop their understanding of sustainable development within the school curriculum,

in particular with their work in geography, science, PSHE [personal, social and health education] and citizenship. (DfEE, 1999)

More detailed guidance for teachers is given on the QCA (Qualifications and Curriculum Authority) website at www.nc.uk.net/esd/index.htm. The equivalent body in Wales has published guidance entitled *Education for Sustainable Development and Global Citizenship* (ACCAC, 2002).

Whilst some educators take education for sustainability to be a fairly recent invention, others point to a longstanding recognition that teachers should help students make sense of global issues. There are three issue-based educations, each with at least a thirty year history, that have provided the building blocks for education for sustainable development (ESD): environmental education, development education, global education (Hicks and Holden, 2007). A wealth of resources is available for educators (Huckle and Sterling, 1996; Smith and Williams, 1999; Stone and Barlow, 2005). It is sources such as these that highlight some of the major debates in the field.

Key issues

Richardson (1986) set out the dilemma when he wrote:

> ...controversy is not to do with different levels of knowledge and information but with different opinions, values and priorities, and, basically and essentially, with different material interests. A controversial issue...is one on which society is divided. The difference of opinion may be about the very definition and naming of the problem to be solved; and/or about its causes and history, in society, in human nature; and/or about the actions which should be taken, both in the short term and long, to remove or manage the problem; and/or about the structure and contours of the ideal situation ... towards which action is taken, and in the utopian light of which the problem was first perceived and labelled. (Richardson, 1986: 17)

The controversies inherent in the notion of education for sustainability thus relate to debates about: i) the meaning of sustainability and ii) the deeper purposes of education.

Meanings of sustainability

The notion of sustainability is deeply contested (Fien and Tilbury, 2003) and the four perspectives outlined below indicate why this is so.

A technocentric perspective

This worldview sees human beings as more important than nature, and technology as the answer to most problems. Technocentrics do not believe major changes are needed in people's lifestyles in order to create a more sustainable society, arguing that problems can be resolved by new technology and government legislation. Technocentrics are reformist in their objectives, believing that economic growth should go on as before – but just in a more sustainable way. Many governments, economists, financiers and business people thus often talk in terms of the need for sustainable growth.

An ecocentric perspective

This is a nature-centred worldview which believes protection of the biosphere is as important as fulfilment of human needs. Natural systems are seen as offering a holistic model of *sustainable development* in which social, economic and environmental goals are of equal importance. Technocentrism is seen as one of the major causes of unsustainable development. Ecocentrics are radical in their objectives, believing major changes in western lifestyles are needed to create a more sustainable society – a view held by most environmentalists, environmental NGOs, younger people and progressive thinkers.

A contrarian perspective

This perspective is held by those who believe environmental issues are *not* a serious cause for concern at all. Contrarians are skeptical about what they consider to be apocalyptic warnings of ecological catastrophe, whether the danger of global warming or the depletion of key mineral resources. This is seen as undue and inappropriate pessimism. Writers like Beckerman (1995) and Lomborg (2001) believe that environmentalists who predict catastrophe do so in order to alarm people and thus increase their revenues and their bureaucracies. Contrarians often work for the fossil fuel industry, big corporations, right-wing think tanks or free-market lobbying groups.

North v. South

The 1992 Earth Summit highlighted major North-South tensions as rich and poor countries of the world saw the problems of sustainability, and solutions, in quite different terms. Northern governments wanted the poorer South to be responsible stewards of the Earth. Southern governments wanted the North to help eradicate poverty. The South saw neocolonialism and the strategies of the International Monetary Fund and World Bank as responsible for unsustainable development. They resented Northern demands that they should not exploit their own natural resources.

So when the term 'sustainability' is used in educational documents it is important to read between the lines in order to assess what definition of sustainability is being offered. It is a contested, and thus controversial, concept.

Education and ideology

Ideology is defined as a broad interlocked set of ideas and beliefs about the world held by a group of people that they demonstrate in both behaviour and conversation to various audiences. These systems of belief are usually seen as 'the way things really are' by the groups holding them, and they become the taken-for-granted way of making sense of the world. (Meighan and Siraj-Blatchford, 2003:186)

One cannot understand the notion of controversy in education without some understanding of political ideology. Goodwin (1997) and Heywood (2005) identify a number of major ideologies in society such as liberalism, conservatism, socialism, feminism and green. Given their taken-for-granted nature it follows that clashes of ideology, political and educational, underlie much of the discussion about the nature of controversial issues. In particular, as Apple (2001) argues, it is neoliberal and neo-conservative ideas which deeply influence education today.

Neoliberalism

The rights of the individual and the attainment of human happiness are the main goals of liberalism. The most important belief for neoliberals is 'economic rationality', i.e. everyone should act to maximise their own personal benefits. Private businesses competing against each other will provide the greatest good for all. Such ideas are part of dominant ideology in the western world. In this worldview money spent on education is seen as a waste unless it helps the country compete effectively in the global market place. Market place metaphors are applied to education: parents as consumers, education as business, internal/external competition to bring out the best in pupils and school. Schools must be modelled on the business world and thus take a more technocratic, managerial and performance driven view of teaching and learning, including sustainability.

Neoconservatism

Conservatives tend to be pessimistic about human nature whilst stressing the importance of tradition, private property and patriotism. Neo-conservatives believe in deregulation of the market in order to encourage competition. 'Free market' economics is seen as the best foundation for a vibrant economy. Neo-conservatives in the UK launched a major attack against the teaching profession in the 1980s and introduced a mandatory national curriculum in order to gain greater control over education. They wanted a return to 'traditional' values, a curriculum untainted by discussion of global issues – such as sustainability – and a stress on higher educational standards. The way to achieve this was felt to be SATs and school league tables. This was based on the belief that competition brings out the best in people and will therefore do the same for both pupils and schools.

Radicalism

Those who take a radical perspective will question the *status quo* in society and the dominant ideologies that support it. They oppose neo-conservative and neoliberal values and see their stress on economic rationality and free market capitalism as one of the main causes of global inequality and debt. The anti-globalisation movement marks a major convergence of radical opposition and brings together a wide range of issues: environment, human rights, debt, poverty, capitalism and transnational corporations (Klein, 2001). Richardson (1990:7) highlights the importance of a radical stance in education when he writes about two long-standing educational traditions, one focusing on the 'person', the other on the 'political'.

> Both ... are concerned with wholeness and holistic thinking, but neither, arguably, is complete without the other. There cannot be wholeness in individuals independently of strenuous attempts to heal rifts and contradictions in wider society and in the education system. Conversely, political struggle to create wholeness in society – that is, equality and justice in dealings and relationships between social classes, between countries, between ethnic groups, between women and men – is doomed to no more than partial success ... if it is not accompanied by ... the search for wholeness and integration in individuals.

This view of education stands in contrast to the dominant ideologies sketched out above. Neoliberal and neoconservative forms of education will tend to focus on the importance of sustainable growth, whilst more progressive and radical forms of education will focus on holistic models of sustainable development.

Climate change

Over the last twenty years climate change has become recognised as one of the major issues affecting the future (Lynas, 2004; IPCC, 2007; Flannery, 2006). Unless greenhouse gases like CO2 occurred naturally there would be no life on Earth since they help trap the heat from the sun. However, human activity has lead to more than 30 per cent increase in CO2 since 1800. This is a result of burning fossil fuels (coal, oil, gas) to create electricity and also using them as a fuel in road, sea and air transport. The consequences are already evident in melting glaciers and ice caps, changes in the seasons, a greater chance of flooding and more extreme weather conditions. As with all issues relating to sustainability, climate change is seen by some as controversial.

Who to believe?

One of the issues at the heart of the climate change debate is the fact that different 'authorities' make opposing claims about its seriousness. Is this then a question of evidence or of ideology or both? Two different perspectives are considered here: i) the international consensus, as represented by the assessment reports of the Intergovernmental Panel on Climate Change; ii) the contrarians, who take a much more skeptical position.

The consensus

Whilst over geological time the average global temperature has ranged from 2C-27C, the average over the last 10,000 years has been 14C. During the course of human history this has only fluctuated by about 1.0C (Flannery, 2006). As a result of increasing CO2 in the atmosphere, the latest increasingly sophisticated climate change simulations estimate that average global temperatures may rise by anything from 1.4 to 11.0C. It has also been calculated that in order to stabilise the Earth's climate, greenhouse gases may need to be cut by as much as 70 per cent. Significant changes in climate have already become apparent over the last twenty years (IPCC, 2007) and the Kyoto Protocol was a vital attempt to reach international agreement over the need to cut carbon emissions. By 2005 enough countries had signed up to this agreement for it to come into force, although not without major debates and disagreements. The two major countries who have refused to sign are the USA and Australia. The USA emits more greenhouse gases per head than any other country, 36 per cent of the world's total.

The skeptics

Australia and the USA have been reluctant to ratify the Kyoto agreement because they fear that the cost of doing so would drastically slow down their rate of economic growth. The seriousness of climate change has been challenged by both the White House and major sectors of American industry, in particular the powerful fossil fuel lobby, i.e. the big coal, oil and gas companies. Some argue that climate change, if it is happening at all, is simply a technological problem and certainly not one that requires a fundamental change in western lifestyles. There is thus a constant questioning of the science behind climate change by powerful lobbying organisations such as the Competitive Enterprise Institute, the American Petroleum Institute, the Heritage Foundation and the Scientific Alliance.

Brown (2005) reports on an investigation into the work of three of the US's most senior climate specialists, which alleged that there were errors in their calculations and demanded details of their funding and of all their publications. Borger and others report incidents of tampering with US climate change research. 'Documents released by a watchdog group ... show that as chief of staff for the White House council on environmental quality, Philip Cooney watered down government scientific papers on climate change and played up uncertainties in the scientific literature. Mr. Cooney is a law graduate and has no scientific training' (Borger, 2005:7). The President of the Royal Society, Robert May, has warned that the UK is likely to be the next ideological battleground for the skeptics (Walsh, 2005). Efforts to establish a European coalition to challenge European Union climate policy are already under way (Adam, 2005).

The controversy

How should one view this controversy? Is it about the nature of the scientific evidence? Is it about two opposing views, both of which deserve equal air time? Is it about which party can put forward the best argument? I fear that many controversial issues may be dealt with in the way of the Literary and Debating Society. The notion here is that two opposing views should be given and debated and that the winner is the person who presents the best argument. I believe this Enlightenment view of rational debate is fundamentally flawed and in this case inappropriate. This deep disagreement about climate change is not just about 'evidence'. It is about different worldviews, i.e. it is about ideological differences.

The consensus view, as reported by the Intergovernmental Panel on Climate Change, comes from the work of innumerable scientists round the world. Whilst skeptics challenge such findings, apparently on scientific grounds, they actually oppose them on ideological grounds – both technocentric and contrarian. This opposition is based on a belief in the primacy of economic growth and the freedom of the individual and business to achieve their own profit-orientated goals. The skeptics are part of a wider grouping of contrarians who oppose all environmental legislation and the environmental movement itself (Rowell, 1996). To know where one stands on this controversy one needs to understand these deeper underlying ideological differences.

In the classroom
In considering the question 'Who to believe?' in the classroom the following pointers may be useful.

- Whilst this may appear to be about a question of evidence, it is also one of ideology
- Initially students could look at short extracts on climate change from the media, scientific reports and lobbying groups
- Question: In what ways are these extracts different from each other? What sort of evidence does each offer about climate change?
- Students are given the source of each extract and asked to consider in what way the source might influence the way in which climate change is described
- The two main ideological interests that could be considered are i) the media's need for a dramatic story and ii) the skeptic's rejection of the problem on technocentric or free-market grounds
- It is important to note that the scientific consensus on climate change is much more powerful than the contrarian lobby. They do not represent two equal sides of an argument.

How to teach?
So how should one approach climate change in the classroom or with student teachers? Whilst there is growing agreement that this issue should be taught about, whether in citizenship, science or geography, much less has been written about a pedagogical controversy that lies at the heart of such issues.

A cognitive perspective

How do educators approach the matter of teaching about global issues? The initial response is often a desire to alert learners to the nature and importance of the problem, whether to do with environment, development, rights or conflict. Geographers, global educators and others have an excellent and long-standing record in relation to this. Two recent examples of materials on climate change are *Climate Chaos: Information for Teachers* (WWF, 2005) and *Climate Change – Local and Global: An Enquiry Approach* (TIDE, 2005). The latter uses an excellent learner-centred approach for investigating global issues. Both are valuable and stimulating resources that I recommend. As I look at them I remember myself as a young teacher in the 1970s, when environmental issues were first appearing in the headlines. I was enthusiastic about introducing students, and later student teachers, to such issues. We looked at the problems and then the solutions and possible action for change.

What I gradually realised was that having explored the problem in depth, my students, both children and adults, often felt so overwhelmed that they were incapable of any action. Perhaps, I wondered, one should teach about the solutions first. Why is wind power one of the fastest growing sources of renewable energy? Why are more and more people buying green electricity? If I got students interested first in such action for change, perhaps they would not feel so overwhelmed by the problem. Most global education materials seem to presume that appropriate enquiry followed by action for change will naturally lead to students feeling more empowered. But this is not necessarily the case.

An affective perspective

What is often missing is the affective dimension. Whilst this is true for much of the curriculum, it matters most when we want students to explore major issues which actually threaten the human condition. Various writers (*inter alia* Beck, 1998) have drawn attention to the uncertainties we face in a 'risk society' and the fears that arise in relation to this. Postel (1992) and others have noted how the overwhelming nature of many global issues drives people into a state of psychic numbing and denial. Eckersley (1999) has observed that the older students are, the more pessimistic they become about the future. To ignore the affective response to climate change is to foreclose on one of the most crucial elements in learning.

One of the best studies on this was carried out by Rogers (1998), who mapped five broad dimensions of learning that she observed in a course on global futures. These were: i) *cognitive dimension*: learning new facts and concepts about global issues; ii) *affective dimension*: all sorts of feelings came up as a result of this – from hopelessness and depression to a sense of challenge; iii) *existential dimension*: for some this led to deep soul-searching about the meaning of life; iv) *empowerment dimension*: if this could be resolved it led to a sense of personal responsibility and commitment; v) *action dimension*: informed personal, social and political action then followed. My own research (Hicks, 2006) on this with undergraduates showed a similar pattern. What ameliorated the initial sense of despair they felt when facing the state of the world was the opportunity to keep a journal recording their responses to the course, and to meet as a group and discuss what they were feeling about the course.

The controversy

The controversy I am highlighting here is, I think, largely unacknowledged. Indeed, many educators would probably argue that a good enquiry based approach to global learning should satisfy all pedagogical demands. To a degree this is true, but it ignores the affect. Cognitive and affective are two sides of the same coin, as work in the field of emotional literacy (Antidote, 2003) fully recognises. The affect is not a missing dimension in education if we are referring to areas such as personal, social and health education (PSHE). I believe it is largely missing, however, in relation to the exploration of global issues such as climate change. This is not helped by the way in which the media report on global warming. Recent headlines such as 'Alarm over dramatic weakening of Gulf Stream', 'Global warming: the 'tipping point'' and 'On the edge: Greenland ice cap breaking up at twice the rate it was five years ago', are disturbing at the very least. If they worry me, then what are students feeling?

Outside of formal education these issues have been addressed in a more holistic and empowering fashion (Macy and Brown, 1998). What young people need to know is that adults are doing something about climate change and that there are things they can do too. They also need the opportunity to share their concerns with adults. As Freire (1994: 9) writes: 'One of the tasks of the progressive educator ... is to unveil opportunities for hope, no matter what the obstacles might be'.

In the classroom

In considering the question 'How to teach?' in the classroom, the following pointers may be useful.

- Begin by asking what it is students feel they know about climate change. This could be done in small groups, with a composite class list then being drawn up. This also enables the teacher to see what incomplete or erroneous information students have

- Follow this by asking students to share in small groups their personal hopes and fears about climate change

- The issue is not whether they are 'unreasonable' hopes and fears in adult terms but rather the need to respect whatever students come up with. The essential task is for students to feel that their concerns have been heard

- It is useful to list fears first and then hopes. It is best to discuss these separately. The teacher's task at this stage is not to try and allay fears but to demonstrate active listening

- If the programme of work that follows acknowledges these hopes and fears, they can be addressed within the on-going context of enquiry

- It is also important to note that statements about the impact of climate change vary according to the time-scale being used. This is not always stated. What might happen in a hundred or 500 years may be dramatic but also beyond the student's own time-frame

- Smaller changes over a few years or decades are less alarming but equally important to consider and equally demanding of local action.

What to do?

Citizenship in particular invites young people to develop their skills of participation and responsible action. At secondary level (DfEE, 1999), 'Pupils should be taught to: a) use their imagination to consider other people's experiences and be able to think about, express and explain views that are not their own; b) negotiate, decide and take part responsibly in both school and community based activities; c) reflect on the process of participating.' What might this look like in relation to climate change? It could be participating in a whole-school project to limit the school's carbon footprint or perhaps taking part in a local or national demonstration against the nuclear industry.

Reformist action

An LEA Inspector told me a few years ago that many of the secondary schools he knew hoped to fulfil the action element of citizenship through work placements, picking up litter and visiting the elderly. This would be a good example of 'modest' action in that it wouldn't require too much effort and, in this case, the school wouldn't have to do anything very differently. This is not to deny that the three examples of action are not each very important in their own right. What then might students be invited to do in relation to climate change? Here are five examples.

- Explain climate change to friends and parents
- Switch off lights voluntarily or when asked
- Make sure that various items are recycled
- Sometimes choose green products when shopping
- Protect trees and green spaces

These actions are all significant because they show an awareness of things that can be done in daily life which will help to reduce carbon emissions. They are all actions which could also be implemented as part of school policy. They are reformist in that they see the problem of climate change as resolvable through a number of small but important changes to the system.

Radical action

More radical action is likely to involve more effort because it will be directed towards changing the system itself. It will require more sustained commitment over a longer period. Here are five examples.

- Go on climate change demonstrations locally or nationally
- Decide to buy electricity from a totally green source
- Challenge unthinking consumerism and materialism
- Shop locally for local produce, e.g. fair-trade/Farmers' Markets
- Plant trees locally and backing such schemes elsewhere
- Use cycle, bus and/or train rather than car or plane when possible

These are also actions that a family or a school can take to help reduce carbon emissions but they will all have a deeper effect than the reformist examples above. Being prepared to go on a local or national demonstration relating to climate change is an act of solidarity with others and a powerful reminder that more can be achieved by working together than alone (www.stopclimatechaos.org). Changing to a green electricity supplier such as Good Energy (www.good-energy.co.uk) will eliminate all carbon emissions from use of electricity at home or at school. Learning to use less of everything, which does not mean sitting in the cold and dark, directly confronts the wasteful materialism and consumerism of western society (www.enough.org.uk). Shopping locally for local products reduces the air miles that many food items travel to reach the supermarket shelves as well as supporting the local economy (www.farmersmarkets.net). Being involved in the work of a Woodland Trust is about taking direct responsibility for the environment in one's own locality and its ability to act as a carbon sink (www.woodland-trust.org.uk). Looking at ways of getting to school without using the car may require a change in lifestyle but it is a healthy one (www.sustrans.org.uk).

The controversy

What then should be the parameters of action for students in school? During the Gulf War some pupils were reprimanded by their schools for going on anti-war demos in school time (*Times Educational Supplement*: 28.03.2003). Should they not have received recognition for their commitment to free speech and democracy? Were they not developing the very skills that citizenship is designed to promote? It is at this point that the word 'political' generally enters the discussion, suggesting that some actions are political whilst others are not. When a headteacher said to me 'I'd be happy to have a speaker from Friends of the Earth at a school assembly, but not Greenpeace', I think this was what he meant. However, this distinction is based on a very narrow meaning of the word politics.

Politics, more broadly, is about issues of power in society, how such power is used and to what ends. Sociologists will therefore talk about the politics of the family, the politics of the workplace and the politics of gender. In this context the whole of education and all of life are inextricably bound up with the politics of everyday life. Some schools will therefore wish to stay on the safe side of any debates about responsible action in the local and global community. Other schools may have a broader vision of such action and ways to promote it. As teachers have repeatedly told me, school councils can be the place where pupils learn about participative democracy or about authoritarian control.

Reflection

In this chapter I have tried to highlight some of the debates that occur – or are waiting to occur – in relation to teaching about global issues. I have done this in relation to the field of education for sustainable development and, more particularly, in relation to issues of climate change. I have indicated, as Richardson (1986) argues, that the very question of whether something is controversial is controversial in itself. My first year students sometimes think that educators should just agree on 'what's best' and then get on with it. A deeper understanding of ideology and educational ideologies shows that there will always be profound differences in the way people view human nature, the appropriate goals of life and the means by which these may be achieved. There will thus always be argument about the purposes of education, the meanings of sustainability and the best way to respond to climate change. Whilst I have simplified the worldviews which underlie these debates, this is not to ignore their complexity and power. Indeed it is educational, political and philosophical ideologies which frame our very sense of what is the norm and what is real. Whether something is controversial or not is at heart not a question of opinion or evidence but rather of one's explicit, or more often implicit, ideological beliefs.

References

ACCAC (2002) *Education for Sustainable Development and Global Citizenship.* Cardiff: Qualifications, Curriculum and Assessment Authority for Wales

Adam, D. (2005) Oil industry targets EU climate policy, *Guardian,* December 8

Antidote (2003) *The Emotional Literacy Handbook.* London: David Fulton

Apple, M. (2001) *Education the 'Right' Way: Markets, Standards, God and Inequality.* London: RoutledgeFalmer

Beck, U. (1998) Politics of risk society, in J. Franklin (ed) *The Politics of Risk Society.* London: Routledge

Beckerman, W. (1995) *Small is Stupid: Blowing the Whistle on the Greens.* London: Duckworth

Borger, J. (2005) Ex-oil lobbyist watered down US climate research, *Guardian,* June 9

Brown, P. (2005) Republicans accused of witch-hunt against climate change scientists, *Guardian*, August 30

DfEE (1999) *The National Curriculum.* London: Department for Education and Employment

Eckersley, R. (1999) Dreams and expectations: young people's expected and preferred futures and their significance for education, *Futures*, 31, pp73-90

Farmers Markets – www.farmersmarkets.net

Fien, J. and Tilbury, D. (2003) The global challenge of sustainability, in D. Tilbury et al. (eds) *Education and Sustainability: Responding to the Global Challenge.* Bern: IUCN (World Conservation Union)

Flannery, T. (2006) *The Weather Makers: The History and Future Impact of Climate Change.* London: Allen Lane

Freire, P. (1994) *Pedagogy of Hope.* London: Continuum

Good Energy – www.good-energy.co.uk

Goodwin, B. (1997) *Using Political Ideas.* Chichester: John Wiley

Heywood, A. (2005) *Political Ideologies*. Basingstoke: Palgrave Macmillan

Hicks, D. (2006) *Lessons for the Future: The Missing Dimension in Education*. Victoria BC: Trafford Publishing

Hicks, D. and Holden, C. (eds) (2007) *The Challenge of Global Education: Key Principles and Effective Practice*. London: RoutledgeFalmer

Huckle, J. and Sterling, S. (eds) (1996) *Education for Sustainability*. London: Earthscan

Intergovernmental Panel for Climate Change, Fourth Assessment Report (2007) – www.ipcc.ch

Klein, N. (2001) *No Logo*. London: Flamingo

Lomborg, B. (2001) *The Skeptical Environmentalist*. Cambridge: Cambridge University Press

Lynas, M. (2004) *High Tide: How Climate Crisis is Engulfing Our Planet*. London: Harper Perennial

Macy, J. and Brown, M. (1998) *Coming Back to Life: Practices to Reconnect Our Lives, Our World*. Gabriola Island BC: New Society Publishers

Meighan, R. and Siraj-Blatchford, I. (2003) *A Sociology of Educating. London:* Continuum

Never Enough? Anti-consumerist Campaign – www.enough.org.uk

Postel, S. (1992) Denial in the decisive decade, chap. 1 in L. Brown and L. Starke (eds) *State of the World 1992*, London: Earthscan

Qualifications and Curriculum Authority – www.nc.uk.net/esd/index.htm

Richardson, R. (1986) The hidden messages of school books, *Journal of Moral Education*, 15 (1), pp26-42

Richardson, R. (1990) *Daring to be a Teacher*. Stoke-on-Trent: Trentham Books

Rogers, M. (1998) Student responses to learning about futures, in D. Hicks and R. Slaughter (eds) (1998) *Futures Education: World Yearbook of Education*. London: Kogan Page

Rowell, A. (1996) *Green Backlash: Global Subversion of the Environmental Movement*, London: Routledge

Smith, G. and Williams, D. (eds) (1999) *Ecological Education in Action*. Albany: State University of New York Press

Stone, M. and Barlow, Z. (eds) (2005) *Ecological Literacy: Educating Our Children for a Sustainable World*. San Francisco: Sierra Club Books

Stop Climate Chaos – www.stopclimatechaos.org

Sustrans – www.sustrans.org.uk

TES (2003) Rebels without a clue? *Times Educational Supplement*, March 28

TIDE (2005) *Climate Change – Local and Global: An Enquiry Approach*. Birmingham: Teachers in Development Education

UN Decade of Education for Sustainable Development – http://portal.unesco.org/education

Walsh, C. (2005) 'Denial lobby' turns up the heat, *Observer*, March 6

Woodland Trust – www.woodland-trust.org.uk

WWF-UK (2005) *Climate Chaos: Information for Teachers*. Godalming: World Wild Life Fund for Education

Teaching the contested and controversial nature of democratic ideas: taking the crisis out of controversy

Andrew Hughes and Alan Sears

In this chapter Andrew Hughes and Alan Sears describe the ideas under-pinning the Spirit of Democracy Project devised and implemented by teacher educators in New Brunswick Canada and the Russian Associa-tion for Civic Education. This involves choosing 'learning situations' from history or current events, which are authentic and multi-dimensional. The children are then guided through a programme to address the con-troversies, perspectives and options which were available at the time and which can be transferred into their contemporary lives.

enerally, if you ask people what they think of abstract ideas like the rule of law, freedom, tolerance, equality, justice or privacy, you are confronted with a blank stare. Yet almost everyone has pas-sionately held views about these ideas – ideas that lie at the core of demo-cratic life. Children often comment that something is 'no fair'. Perhaps it's taking turns or a younger child being sent to bed earlier than a sibling but the ungrammatical utterance conveys a theory of justice; the child knows that there is a principle that has been violated. Eavesdrop on friends or neighbours discussing the extended incarceration without charge of terrorist suspects. They might not refer to the rule of law or Magna Carta, but the concepts certainly inform their perspectives and in context, be-come vibrant, living examples of the principles that we want to shape our societies. It is only the abstract issues which evoke the blank stare.

Sometimes it can seem that society is in crisis, because of the scale of current controversies. In this chapter we describe an approach which aims to take the crisis out of controversy, by setting contentious ideas in a social and historical context. For example, we can look at historical cases related to freedom of speech, before drawing analogies with contemporary situations. Or we can explore affirmative action, or occasions when government withdrew civil rights in times of crisis.

The ideas of democracy often knock heads and struggle for precedence: does security trump freedom? How do we balance the will of the majority and the rights of the minority? Young people need an opportunity to see that the ideas of democracy are contested and fluid, do not take the same form everywhere and can be worked out in different ways. Democracy is possible in monarchies and republics, federations and unitary states, through proportional representation or first past the post, unicameral and bicameral legislatures; it can be inclusive and sometimes exclusive. Political philosophers may debate these ideas in the abstract but ordinary people draw on real situations.

Our challenge, as educators, is to help young people see and assess these shifting embodiments of democracy. The problems of living peaceably together today, are not identical to a generation ago, nor will they apply exactly in the next generation. The next generation, however, needs to be able to draw on analogies, and to have practised enlightened thinking about the issues, moving from concrete instances towards abstraction.

The Spirit of Democracy Project

During the past six years teacher education tutors at the University of New Brunswick in Canada have been collaborating with colleagues at the Russian Association for Civic Education on a programme that thrusts young people into confrontation with the ideas of democracy. The Spirit of Democracy Project (www.spiritofdemocracy.com) builds opportunities for learning around historical situations. They are intended to open up elements of democratic living that are regularly contested and in conflict. Sometimes these serve as anchors, providing a common frame of reference for discussion; sometimes they are springboards, launching further exploration. Children of all ages, with the guiding hand of their teachers, can explore issues ranging from the value of a free press to the meaning of loyalty, from the limits of tolerance to the nature of respect.

First, we bring pupils into contact with an idea, and provoke a gut reaction. Then we push them towards deeper and extended understanding of other people's as well as their own conceptions. We do this through learning situations that children already meet through the regular school curriculum. We use this situation as a springboard to launch into a further examination of the ideas, in other contexts. We aim to move beyond mere activity and experience towards what we have called a learning experience. Vygotsky's framework for interpersonal and intrapersonal learning serves us well: our approach displays the hallmarks of his notion of situated learning. Thought and action is located in a specific place and time; significant others – both proximal and distal – are engaged in the process with the learner (Lave and Wenger, 1991).

Learning situations

Suitable situations or contexts for exploring ideas can emerge from ordinary everyday life. Often however, they come from the regular school curriculum. The following examples show what we mean by situations or contexts, or metaphorically by anchors or springboards.

Children typically learn about the franchise – from the expansion of suffrage for adult male property owners to universal suffrage. But in the words of a Canadian study, the history they learn consists of 'nice, neat, little acts of Parliament' (Hodgetts, 1968:19). This is important information. Our children should know it. But how do we help them acquire it? In-depth examination of a particular episode often helps pupils connect with the concepts where previously they just learned the facts.

Consider the following episode:

On Tuesday, March 10, 1914, a Canadian woman, Mary Richardson, entered the National Gallery in London, went to Velasquez's masterpiece, the Rokeby Venus, and

> . . . producing a meat chopper from her muff or cloak, smashed the glass of the picture, and rained blows upon the back of the Venus. A police officer was at the door of the room, and a gallery attendant also heard smashing of the glass. They rushed towards the woman, but before they could seize her she had made seven cuts in the canvas.

> She was immediately arrested with the police report indicating that she had been involved in 'similar outrages' including smashing store windows and arson. (*Manchester Guardian*, 1914)

Mary Richardson was a suffragette and saw her actions as no more outrageous than British society's oppression of women. In explaining her actions she wrote,

> I have tried to destroy the picture of the most beautiful woman in mytho-
> logical history as a protest against the Government destroying Mrs. Pank-
> hurst, who is the most beautiful character in modern history ... Justice is
> an element of beauty as much as colour and outline on canvas. Mrs.
> Pankhurst seeks to secure justice for womanhood, and for this she is be-
> ing slowly murdered by a Government of Iscariot politicians. (*Guardian*,
> 2003)

Like adults, children find this story and its implications intriguing. What does this painting look like? Can we still see it today? Why this particular painting? Who was Mrs. Pankhurst? What was happening to her? Why? What are 'Iscariot politicians'? The facts reach out and grab the pupils' attention. And what of the ideas embedded in the story: the right to dissent, civil disobedience, equality, the meaning of 'consent of the governed'? The episode provides the opportunity to go beyond the facts – to explore the ideas, to assess our personal positions, to test our views against those of others.

This event happened long ago and is far removed from the direct experience of children in Canada and Russia – or indeed the UK – but it is relevant and telling. It provides pupils with a springboard to explore their own sense of how the world is and how it might be. They can write letters to the *Guardian's* editor, serve as prosecutor, defence counsel or jury member at Mary Richardson's trial, or compose a dialogue that begins 'Good day Ms. Richardson, I've always wanted to talk to you about that business with the Rokeby Venus'. They not only reflect specifically on this case but also explore their views on handling matters of dissent and consent in our modern societies.

We use this episode as an anchor, a context for students to engage with and to confront their own sense of legitimacy and justice in society. As they engage with contested concepts, they learn that well-informed people may see the world differently. British people in the early twentieth century subscribed broadly to the notion that government should function according to the will of the people. However, Richardson's contemporaries typically excluded anyone but adult white, property owning males from their notion of 'the people'. Pupils now examine the origins and evolution of such ideas; they explore the consistencies and the conflicts; they assess the relevance of differing conceptions in the past, to their own, contemporary societies.

Consent of the governed is a core idea of democracy, but who gives consent and how it is manifested are contested within and between societies. In order to participate actively in the pursuit of resolutions, pupils need to know the detail of specific episodes. Thus, contested ideas are made concrete, and they come face to face with the conflicts and challenges.

Selecting episodes – the critical attributes

Most of the episodes we use as learning situations are drawn from actual historical or current events, as with the Mary Richardson story. Contrived situations are not nearly as compelling as reality, though occasionally we use a fictionalised version of an actual event. The teacher needs to recognise the learning potential in subject matter, going beyond the facts to the ideologies and values that shape them. For example, systems of taxation include ideas of fraternity and responsibility; free speech incorporates ideas of respect; Magna Carta or the Great Reform Bill are about the rule of law. The juxtaposition of details and ideas tacitly acknowledges Kant's dictum that concepts without percepts are empty, and percepts without concepts are blind (Kant, 1965).

We have identified six attributes that are crucial to a successful teaching situation and use them as design specifications for identifying, selecting and creating particular episodes. Each situation must be:

- authentic
- vividly rendered
- succinct
- multi-dimensional
- deliberately ambiguous
- representative

Authentic situations are those where real people confront real dilemmas.

Vivid rendering means that the issues in a situation should stand out in stark relief. With Mary Richardson, the issue is not simply one of dissent. It also embraces illegal action and overt violence. Pupils confront an instance of breaking the law and acting violently – possibly not their idea of how to express dissent. But how would they have acted in Mary Richardson's shoes? Can they conceive of situations today where they might support illegal or violent action? How do they think we should respond to those who act violently and/or illegally in order to promote a political cause?

Succinct episodes means we do not need to know the full background, but should be able to engage with the situation on its own merits. People usually, have no difficulty in forming a view about Mary Richardson and the Rokeby Venus. They don't require an introductory lecture on the suffragettes or women's rights in order to form an opinion. The situation itself is only part of the learning opportunity; ideas and concepts are contained within it. It is a springboard to launch pupils into considering issues that transcend the particular circumstances.

The Russian teachers we work with often make use of important cultural artefacts such as the painting *The Old Believer* by Boyarynya Morozova. This is a nineteenth century portrayal of a seventeenth century event, in which a woman belonging to a banned sect was carried off to prison for her beliefs. Most Russian children recognise the painting and know the associated story. Their teachers use it as a springboard to launch a study of religious freedom, starting with seventeenth century Russia, moving into the nineteenth century, then the new Russia of the 21st century, and finally the wider world. Pupils explore a variety of ideas though this springboard, a single painting. Both rational and emotional responses can emerge as their understanding is deepened.

Multidimensional situations allow for and encourage pupils to consider ideas at a number of levels and from different perspectives. Mary Richardson was seen by her contemporaries as both outrageous and heroic; *The Old Believer* was the object of both sympathy *and* scorn. The facts behind the chosen situations have intrinsic interest but their value lies in projecting pupils beyond the information given, through exploring ideas of equality and dissent, freedom and respect.

Ambiguity enhances the potential for learning and is related to multidimensionality. For a situation to work it has to be open-ended and open to interpretation. For example, if Mary Richardson were viewed universally as a violent anti-social criminal, our consideration of her place in history would be limited. But some people believe that she was far-sighted, self-sacrificing and heroic.

Representative situations should include ideas and concepts that are common across a number of situations and not limited to the specific episode. These should contribute to our understanding of our world and should have relevance to pupils' contemporary world. Mary Richardson's story mirrors features of dissent found in many contexts today; persecution for religious nonconformity is not unique to seventeenth century Russia.

Engaging situations

This subtitle is deliberately ambiguous. It can refer to situations that are interesting and appealing or to coming to grips with a situation. Once the learning potential in school subject matter is recognised, the teacher must decide what to do so that the material becomes a genuine learning situation.

A pedagogy to support learning through engaging situations

A variety of learning activities can achieve these goals: some for pupils to pursue independently and some with the teacher's guidance. We try to structure the pedagogy to reflect Vygotsky's view that the child's cultural development occurs on two planes: first, on the social level, and later, on the individual level (Vygotsky, 1978). This requires collaborative learning (*inter-personal* learning). The possibilities are then weighed, accepted, altered, discarded by the pupils themselves (*intra-personal* learning).

Vygotsky notes that inter-personal communication can be more than conversation with one's peers and contemporaries. It can – and should – involve interaction with our collective history and culture – books, articles, films, works of art and virtual environments. Educated pupils will be aware of more than the ideas of their peers and immediate teachers: they will also have engaged with the ideas of the world's best thinkers from different eras and places. As teachers, our challenge is to connect our pupils with this thinking and to design learning activities that will help them engage with those ideas.

Our pupils are not some kind of Aristotelian blank slate. They come with preconceptions and the challenge is to move them beyond these existing understandings, which may be limited, biased or prejudiced. Even when they follow the rules of discussion and debate, classroom exchanges between pupils risk being no more than 'democratic idle talk ... aimless, undocumented chitchat' (Hodgetts, 1968:18). The pedagogy we suggest is an adaptation of methods of 'cognitive apprenticeship' (Weigel, 2002).

Modelling

In modelling we try to assist the learner to develop a mental image or conceptual model of a cognitive process or an idea. This means making visible something that is not usually open to direct observation. For example, we are not able to see directly what is going on when someone is comparing and contrasting, or making an inference, or developing an hypothesis. The challenge is to bring processes out into the open so that students can observe, and practise (Yam San Chee, 1995). One important technique is 'thinking aloud'. While the teacher performs a task she verbalises her thought processes. For example, she talks through the steps involved in decision-making. Also useful is Vygotsky's advice to draw on cultural artefacts such as historical records which describe how particular decisions were reached, for example, a letter written for political purposes, such as Einstein's letters to President Roosevelt about the atomic bomb, or 'J'Accuse!', Zola's famous letter to the President of the French Republic about the Dreyfus case. Either can help pupils consider aspects of political participation. They can analyse the letters and use them as models for composing letters on topics of their own choosing. Thus we can move beyond the empty rhetoric of 'right to participate', and help pupils learn how to participate, while considering responsibility, obligation and repercussions.

Coaching and mentoring

Coaching and mentoring help pupils shape new skills and ideas. In this stage they make new knowledge their own: they assimilate and accommodate it into their own intellectual schemata. The teacher can use feedback, cueing, questioning, correcting, cajoling, supporting, encouraging, mimicking and modelling, visualising and adapting. Coaching and mentoring relate to the task at hand, such as using the fingers to play a trumpet, but they can also support the transfer of ideas and skills from one context to another. For example, pupils learning the basic skill of structuring an argument can apply this to the task of writing a letter to a newspaper or making a submission to a commission of inquiry. The teacher requires keen powers of observation and the ability to give feedback in a way the pupil can receive.

Scaffolding

If you have ever taught a child to swim or to ride a bike, you already know about scaffolding. It means providing the support and the structure for learners to do something they could not do by themselves. Scaffolding has significant roles in pupils' learning:

- It provides emotional, technical and conceptual support
- It extends the learner's range
- It allows the learner to accomplish a task not otherwise possible
- It is used selectively to aid the learner when they need it

- It functions as a cognitive tool assisting the learner to develop a schema for an idea or operation that exceeds their independent grasp
- It allows them to grow into an idea or ability, and on removal, reduces dependence on a more capable other.

Scaffolding helps us to reach an understanding that we might not otherwise achieve; the teacher's task is to assess what a pupil needs and then provide an appropriate and relevant scaffold. These may be graphic organisers such as concept maps, or metaphors and analogies which help pupils make connections. Our Russian colleagues use the analogy of a parent reading a teenager's diary to consider the citizen's right to privacy. The diary example offers a springboard into a wider consideration of privacy in the workplace or public places.

Articulation
Articulation means converting what is often tacit and implicit so that it becomes explicit and subject to scrutiny. It can involve internal self-talk but can also mean articulating mental images and operations or the expression of ideas in words. It can also take the form of non-linguistic, visual representations such as concept maps and mind maps. Articulation is relevant both to learning and teaching – for instance when someone says 'I know what it is ... I just can't put it into words' and the teacher supports her with the task.

In order to describe, compare and contrast, critique, assess or analyse, summarise or synthesise, you have to be able to verbalise. The key element in all these tasks is that thinking must move from the private world into the public world, culminating in a performance or product that can be examined by others. For example, pupils can represent their ideas about key concepts in posters, plays, cartoons or concept maps. Asked to illustrate the relationship between the state and the people in a democracy, a Russian pupil drew an hourglass with an eye at the central point. She said the sand represented the state which had to pass through the eye of the people to move through the hourglass. For her, a key aspect of a democracy was scrutiny of state activities by the people.

Reflecting
When someone reflects, they compare their own perspective, judgment or decision with those of other people. The metaphor implies that light is thrown on the object of discussion. As an intellectual activity, the learner

must compare themselves with a peer or more capable other. Through this comparison learners consider how their performance or product differs, and what these differences imply. They might judge that their performance or product reached the standard of recognised authorities, and their confidence would be boosted. If they noted that their own or others' work was deficient, they would have a model for improvement. The pupils reflect: the teacher debriefs.

One of the goals of the reflecting process is to nurture pupils' insights into their own experience by skilful debriefing. They will almost invariably have learned more from any experience than they at first realise. Reflection draws on Vygotsky's concept of intra-personal dialogue. Having considered what 'knowledgeable others' think of a situation or idea, pupils then clarify and assess their own thinking. For example, in a recent case before the Supreme Court of Canada, a school board argued its right to exclude from schools a child's book that portrayed a gay family. Much of the argument made in Court addressed issues of censorship and age appropriateness. The Chief Justice declared that 'tolerance is always age appropriate' (*Chronicle Herald*, 2002).

Having examined the arguments, pupils must reflect on their own positions. Whether the issue relates to children's books in 21st century Canada or the conflict about the solar system between Galileo and Pope Urban VIII in 17th century Europe, they struggle with ideas such as censorship and the free flow of ideas.

Exploring

Exploring as a method of teaching and learning is associated with cognitive apprenticeship. The teacher pushes pupils toward independent learning, not just in developing resolutions, but in setting the problems themselves. The teacher may propose a general direction for learning, but the pupils are encouraged to select the issues for examination, frame the specific questions and propose the hypotheses for testing. For example, after thinking about dissent in the context of the Suffragettes, students might investigate where dissent is apparent in their own communities, its causes and how it is dealt with.

Weigel (2002) has linked such exploring to what he calls the 'skill' of curiosity. How can the non-curious be expected to take the risks associated with exploring? This is where our strategies come into their own; exploring and curiosity are fostered by the techniques of modelling, coaching, scaffolding, articulating and reflecting.

Conclusion

When we first started to work with the Russian Association for Civic Education on the Spirit of Democracy Project in 1999, a Russian television interviewer asked us why we thought that democracy was the best form of government for Russia. We replied that we did not hold strong views about the best form of government for Russia. However, as educators, we did have strong views that decisions should be informed by clear conceptions of the possibilities. We believe that such clear conceptions are developed by a citizenry who, as pupils, has had the opportunity to consider how contested democratic ideas have been understood and applied over time and across contexts, and who has reflected on how they should be worked out in their own context.

References

Chee, Y.S. (1995) Cognitive apprenticeship and its application to the teaching of small-talk in a multimedia interactive learning environment, *Instructional Science*, 23, pp133-161

Chronicle-Herald (2002) Top Court: School Board in B.C. Unjustified in Banning Books, December 21

Guardian (2003) Big Brother and the Sisters, October 10

Hodgetts, A.B. (1968) *What Culture? What Heritage? A Study of Civic Education in Canada.* Toronto: OISE Press.

Kant, I. (1965) *Critique of Pure Reason*, New York: St Martin's Press

Lave, J. and Wenger, E. (2003) *Situated Learning: Legitimate Peripheral Participation*, Cambridge: Cambridge University Press

Manchester Guardian (1914) Suffragette Outrage, March 11

Vygotsky, L.S. (1978) *Mind and Society: The Development of Higher Mental Processes.* Cambridge, MA: Harvard University Press

Weigel, Van B. (2002) *Deep Learning for a Digital Age: Technology's Untapped Potential to Enrich Higher Education*, San Francisco: Jossey-Bass

'Should the hijab be allowed in school?' a structured approach to tackling controversial issues with older students

Anne Sliwka

In this chapter Anne Sliwka describes her work with secondary aged students in Germany who selected the controversies they wished to debate, researched the issues and, using the experiential methodology of 'deliberation fora', presented their case to an audience of their peers. She argues for rethinking both the structure and pedagogy of the curriculum to make space for an integrated vision of democracy.

The Deliberation Project

German schools at upper secondary level are gradually introducing new settings for learning which provide students with opportunities to work in heterogenous groups, act autonomously and use resource material interactively. These three skill areas have been identified by the OECD's DeSeCo Study (Rychen and Salganik, 2003) as key competences schools need to develop in order to prepare young adults for a society characterised by increasing societal diversity and demanding flexibility and lifelong learning.

The deliberation forum, an innovative setting for learning developed in response to these new demands, promises to develop all three of these competences. Inspired by empirical research on deliberative democracy conducted in the field of political science (Fishkin, 1991; Fishkin, 1995; Bohmann and Regh, 1997; Bohmann, 2000), we created a setting in which students can learn about and deliberate on controversial issues in a structured environment. In this chapter, I describe how this approach can be used by others and critically reflect on our work with students aged 15 to 18 on self-chosen controversial subjects.

After a trial forum at a summer school for gifted students, deliberation fora took place in four German secondary schools in the cities of Karlsruhe, Berlin, Hamburg and Freiburg (Sliwka, 2004). The students in three of the schools were twelfth grade (age 17 or 18) and chose the deliberation project as an elective course. These courses have been introduced to provide opportunities for interdisciplinary and experiential learning to prepare students for higher education. Students have three additional 45-minute lessons per week and the work is assessed, contributing to their final GPA, thus providing a real incentive to work hard. In the fourth school, teachers of English, German and history planned the project cooperatively and implemented it over a course of lessons with tenth grade students.

The Deliberation Project: a three-stage process
First stage: choosing a controversial issue and preparing the questionnaire

In a deliberation project, a group of students, the project group, first has to select a controversial issue that other students might find interesting to debate in the forum. Students compile a list of controversial issues and then vote on which they want to deal with. Not surprisingly, they tend to choose topics different from those their teachers might have selected for them, as the issues chosen to date illustrate:

- Germany's immigration policy
- The extent to which civil rights should be limited in the fight against terrorism.
- Turkey's membership of the EU
- Ethical questions concerning genetic engineering

Information on the issue chosen is generally readily available in the media, in recently published books, newspapers and magazines as well as on the Internet. In the first few weeks students conduct extensive research on their chosen controversial issue, dividing it into its individual aspects and preparing a survey questionnaire. Each questionnaire contains two different types of questions: those testing knowledge about the issue and those surveying opinions or attitudes about it. The early phase of the project stimulates substantial cognitive learning as students discover that most controversial issues consist of several sub-issues. The broad topic of immigration policy, for example, contained sub-questions like 'Should women teachers be allowed to wear the hijab (Muslim headscarf)?' or 'Should German language lessons followed by a language exam be mandatory for all immigrants to Germany?'

Most sub-issues allow for more than just two alternative opinions, as is apparent in the following question from the questionnaire on immigration. For this project group, one out of six controversial sub-issues on immigration concerned the wearing of the hijab in German schools. The overall question was framed as follows:

> Hijabs in German state schools: Which legal option do you prefer? Please rank your answers in order of preference:
>
> A) Neither female teachers nor female students should be allowed to wear the hijab in schools.
>
> B) Female teachers should not be allowed to wear the hijab in school, but female students may do so.
>
> C) Female students under the age of 18 should not be allowed to wear the hijab, but students over the age of 18 and teachers may do so.
>
> D) Both female teachers and female students should be allowed to wear the hijab in schools.

The example shows that one of the first and perhaps most challenging tasks for the students is to identify the sub-issues of the controversial issue and then list possible answers or preferences concerning the specific sub-issues. This requires logical thinking, as all potential answers or preferences have to be mutually exclusive and completely exhaustive so that no viable options are left out and the survey offers all the possible answers. Identifying the logical structure behind a controversial issue may be the first step in appreciating the complexity of such issues.

Luskin, Fishkin and Jowell (2002), in their analysis of data of so-called deliberative polls with randomly chosen adults, showed that deliberation enhances a meta-consensus about controversial issues, namely a consensus about the logical structure of an unstructured and seemingly messy controversy. Our research indicates that exploring an issue with a structured questionnaire helps students understand the various dimensions of a controversial issue (List and Swilka, 2004). This may be a necessary precondition for understanding that complex problems cannot be solved by thinking in terms of black and white. Students come to understand that knowledge of the selected issue can be tested by specific questions in the questionnaire, where respondents are provided with a range of different answers, only one of which is actually correct. A knowledge question asked in the deliberation project on immigration policy, for example, was 'What percentage of individuals seeking political asylum in Germany in 2002 was granted political asylum?'

Second stage: organising and managing a deliberation forum

After preparing the questionnaire to cover both opinions and knowledge, the project group organises the deliberation forum. In the case study schools, about 80 to 100 students from the same school and in one case students from a neighbouring school were invited to learn and deliberate about the controversial issue over two full school days.

Each forum follows a similar pattern. Before it starts, participating students are asked to fill in the anonymous and coded questionnaires. After submitting their questionnaires, the participants enter the hall and are welcomed by two students from the project group. Two others introduce the controversial issue chosen for the forum. Experience has shown that a PowerPoint presentation strictly limited to basic factual information on the controversial issue is most effective.

The presentation is followed by a panel of 'experts', typically academics or professionals whose work relates to the controversial issue. They give eight to ten-minute presentations, followed by question-and-answer sessions, facilitated by another pair of students from the project group.

After a break, the participants are arranged in groups of 8 to10 students for further deliberation. Each deliberation group is facilitated by one of the project group, who has been taught group facilitation skills in preparation for this. They lead the groups through the same issues as those in the questionnaire. Speaking cards can be used to scaffold the interaction and help ensure that all the participants contribute equally to the deliberation process. Each participant is given three speaking cards and two question cards, one of which must be passed to the facilitator whenever they wish to contribute to the deliberation process or ask another participant a question. Facilitators can hand out new speaking cards once all participants' cards have been used up. After about two hours of group deliberation, all participants meet again in a plenary session to conclude the first day with brief presentations by the facilitators on the deliberation results of their respective groups.

On the second day, students reconvene in the hall to listen to a panel of politicians from all political parties. To our surprise, it was not a problem to get politicians to contribute. Competition between political parties apparently worked in our favour as many politicians agreed to come when they discovered that representatives of opposing parties were participating. In addition, adolescents seem to be an interesting audience for politicians, who like to gain the attention of first-time voters.

As with the experts on the first deliberation day, each of the politicians is given eight to ten minutes to present a party view on the controversial issue at stake. This too is followed by a question-and-answer session facilitated by two of the project group. As on the first day, participants are randomly assigned to new deliberation groups. In the final plenary the deliberation results are summed up by the project group facilitators.

At the end of the forum, participating students are asked to complete the questionnaire again. Both the pre and post-forum-questionnaires should be coded so that knowledge and opinions can be compared before and after the forum. This completes the second phase of the project.

Third stage: analysing data and presenting results
After the forum, the project group's main task is to analyse the survey data to identify attitude changes as well as changes in knowledge. They may use software such as Excel and SPSS. The project group prepares a final presentation for all participating students and teachers where they explain the extent to which knowledge and opinions have changed as a result of the forum. This is also a chance for project group members to reflect on their own learning over the course of the project.

Critical reflections on the project
Student outcomes
Our evaluation of the four deliberative fora indicates that this innovative learning setting has the potential to achieve a wide range of pedagogical aims. The experiences of the groups of students involved differ:

i) *students in the project groups*

These students benefited from the experience in multiple ways (Sliwka, 2004). Most said it was the first time in their school career that they had worked in a project as interactive as this, learning that in order to achieve a result from a complex task each was dependent on the others. The tasks the students were in charge of were wide ranging. They included: deciding on the controversial issue, researching the broader issue at stake, developing the questionnaire, organising the forum – a task that required project management methods and skills – facilitating the panel plenary sessions and small deliberation groups, analysing the data and preparing a presentation on knowledge gains and attitude changes. Ninety-seven per cent of the students (n=64) surveyed thought they had learned new skills valuable for their future professional lives; 94 per cent said they had successfully worked in teams and 88 per cent stated that this was the first time they had completed a long-term project in a team. All the students in the project groups developed significant expertise on the issue at stake, as was evident through analysis of student essays.

ii) *students in the audience – the participants*

As indicated by the participants' responses in the pre- and post-forum questionnaires, all four deliberation projects caused attitudes to change. However, these changes were slight (12 to 18 per cent on average) compared to the significant changes in their knowledge about the controversial issues. Few participants answered many knowledge questions correctly before the forum (12 – 34 per cent) but 80 to 100 per cent of answers were correct after the event. Research on expertise (Bereiter and Scardamalia, 1993) confirms what our study suggests: that knowledge is a necessary precondition for making sense of complex controversial issues.

Learning settings for teaching controversial issues thus need to be knowledge-rich environments which enable students to develop expertise on the topic. The responses of the students to some of the controversial issues chosen indicates that their understanding is very much shaped by individual soundbites of information they pick up from the media rather than any kind of connected knowledge or expertise. The outcomes of the fora showed the potential of the discussions to help students think more deeply about the various aspects of complex topics.

Deliberation also seems to increase students' ability to understand perspectives, attitudes and opinions different from their own. After the deliberation forum on immigration issues, far more of the German students said they had better understanding of why some Muslim students decide to wear the hijab. Our experience with all four deliberative fora shows that this teaching strategy has the potential to stimulate significant student interest in controversial issues. Such interest and motivation can be a starting point for more detailed classroom work on the historic, economic, social and cultural backgrounds to the issues discussed. Students can thus develop more thorough and complex understandings.

Teaching styles

Teaching controversies in interdisciplinary, project-based settings involving large numbers of students works best when teachers cooperate in working with the project group. Wherever several teachers with their respective subject expertise scaffolded the students' learning process over the course of the project, students benefited from the new interdisciplinary and experiential learning process. Teachers who deliberately applied the cognitive apprenticeship model (Collins *et al*, 1989) and were able to support students in the project group by flexibly using the teaching strategies of modelling, coaching, scaffolding and reflection achieved the best learning results and the highest student satisfaction. This highlights the need for teacher educators to prepare teachers to use such approaches.

The German context

Finally I reflect on the impact that a project like the deliberative fora has on school structure and school development and analyse some of the structural and cultural challenges encountered.

Until recently, teaching in German schools has been a comparatively isolated undertaking. Teachers plan their teaching strategies at home – often on their own. They do not have offices or networked computers in the school, and the idea of a 'professional learning community' (Dufour and Eaker, 1998) is unknown. Secondary school teachers tend to define themselves as subject specialists rather than experts on learning or as school developers. The professional language they speak is shaped by their subject identity and often fragments rather than unites the school's teaching body. German schools have traditionally been rather inward-looking, and most principals would not regard the need to tap into resources outside the school as a priority.

The four projects reveal the potential for change. The outside world is clearly ready to support schools in organising stimulating learning enquiries. Most of the professionals involved in implementing the deliberation projects were surprised at the interest and willingness of both experts and politicians to come to the schools to contribute their expertise to the deliberation process.

As Michael Fullan (1993) has pointed out, school structures and the school culture are interdependent. Therefore, any sustainable innovation process needs to tackle both simultaneously. In the long run, new experiential learning settings like the deliberation project are unlikely to pass the stage of superficial initiation – limited to only a few actors in a school – unless school autonomy, along with professional school leadership and a national framework for citizenship education, leads to a much more comprehensive strategy for change. Senior management in schools needs to take responsibility for infusing an integrated vision of democracy throughout the curriculum. Fortunately, the new competence-based and outcome-oriented educational standards in German education provide a much better framework for experiential civic learning of the kind introduced in this chapter than the previous curricula, which narrowly defined subject content. As other European countries look to introduce more creative approaches to learning in general and more effective routes to citizenship in particular (QCA, 2004; LOE, 2005) it is to be hoped that this model from Germany will offer inspiration and encouragement.

References

Bereiter, C. and Scardamalia, M. (1993) *Surpassing ourselves: An inquiry into the nature and implications of expertise.* La Salle, IL: Open Court

Bohman, J. (2000) *Public Deliberation, Pluralism, Complexity and Democracy.* Cambridge, Ma: MIT Press

Bohman, J. and Rehg, W. (Hrsg.) (1997) *Deliberative Democracy: Essays on Reason and Politics.* Cambridge, MA: MIT Press

Collins, A., Brown, J.S. and Newman, S. E. (1989) Cognitive Apprenticeship: Teaching the Crafts of Reading, Writing, and Mathematics, in: Resnick, L.B. (Hrsg.) *Knowing, Learning and Instruction. Essays in honour of Robert Glaser.* Hillsdale: Erlbaum.

DuFour, R. and Eaker, R. (1998) *Professional Learning Communities at Work. Best Practices for Enhancing Student Achievement.* Bloomington, Indiana: National Education Service

Fishkin, J. S. (1991) *Democracy and Deliberation.* New Haven: Yale University Press

Fishkin, J. S. (1995) *The Voice of the People.* New Haven: Yale University Press

Fullan, M. (1993) *Change Forces.* London: Routledge

List, C. and Sliwka, A. (2004) Deliberative Polling als Methode zum Erlernen des demokratischen Sprechens, in: *Zeitschrift für Politik*, März

LOE (2005) *Anteproyecto de Ley Orgánica de Educación.* 30 de marzo, Madrid: Ministerio de Educación y Cultura

Luskin, R. C., Fishkin, J. S. and Jowell, R. (2002) Considered Opinions: Deliberative Polling in Britain, *British Journal of Political Science* 32 (3), pp455-487

QCA (2004) *Creativity: find it, promote it.* London; QCA

Rychen, D.S. and Salganik, L.H. (2003) *Key Competencies for a Successful Life and a Well-Functioning Society,* Göttingen: Hogrefe and Huber

Sliwka, A. (2004): Das Deliberationsforum als neue Form des politischen Lernens in der Schule, in: *Kursiv – Journal für Politische Bildung*, October.

Teaching about a controversial electoral system: lessons from Japan

Norio Ikeno

In this case study from Japan, Professor Norio Ikeno describes a project where Japanese students debated the merits of different electoral systems, in the context of the current controversy about representation in Japan.

The approach through which the students engaged with the issues, and the way they distinguished between facts and values, and learned to engage in rational argument, is easily transferable to other contexts and issues.

This chapter describes a project undertaken by Japanese Junior High students to debate a currently controversial issue in Japanese politics, namely the pros and cons of a mixed electoral system combining first past the post with proportional representation.

Forty-five students aged 14-15 in a ninth grade civics course at a private Japanese Junior High school took part in the project in 2003. In most Japanese Junior High schools, social studies comprise geography and history in the seventh and eighth grades, and civics in the ninth grade. Civics is intended to educate young adults for good citizenship. The civics courses cover the political, economic, social and cultural aspects of society, including institutional frameworks and the political, moral and economic ideas which support them. I believe that civics education in Japan could be improved if students critically considered the structure of society, thinking about how to reformulate society's rules and institutions. I draw upon Popper and Kato's premise that students should think critically about the notion of a 'good society' and how the electoral system might promote this (Popper, 1987; Kato, 2003).

To promote such critical thinking, the sessions in the case study classroom were organised to exemplify principles of legitimate rationality in critical communication theory (Habermas, 1981). They aimed to:

- distinguish the facts from the claims and values
- structure the teaching content according to Toulmin's model for structuring an argument (Toulmin, 2003)
- ensure that the controversies are part of the structure of argument through identifying the conflict inherent in the issue
- construct the stages necessary for understanding the nature of the controversies
- evaluate student outcomes
- identify progress in the students' stages of understanding.

Toulmin's model for structuring an argument follows a DCWB pattern:

D – Data	What are the facts about the electoral system?
C – Claim	How far does the system lead to a good democratic society?
W – Warrant	A description of the principles of such a society.
B – Backing	Citing an exemplary society and its properties.

Before describing the sessions, I offer a strategy for teaching about controversial issues within the civics curriculum. It entails identifying and exploring plural perspectives.

Stage 1: select a controversial issue

Stage 2: structure arguments about the issue, using Toulmin's model (set out above)

Stage 3: structure other arguments and make links

Stage 4: broadly judge the issue from various perspectives, and propose ideas for a 'good' democratic society.

I have described elsewhere (Ikeno *et al*, 2004) how students are encouraged to distinguish between facts, claims and values, and structure their arguments to make any conflicts of interest transparent. Here I describe the details of the project in which students debated the pros and cons of different electoral systems, comparing and contrasting systems in place elsewhere in the world with the Japanese situation, and evaluating the benefits of each.

The controversy: the electoral system in Japan

There are opposing opinions about the electoral system in Japan. Previously, in a so-called 'medium constituency' system, a few representatives were elected in an electoral district. Several electoral districts made up a prefecture. The area of the districts under this system was larger than under the single-seat electoral district system, but smaller than in a 'major constituency' system. 'A medium constituency' system operated in Japan for about 50 years after WWII. In recent years the system was changed to a combination of single-seat first past the post, together with proportional representation. Public opinion has been divided over the pros and cons of the new mixed system.

Objectives

Students should be able to identify and set out the underlying principles of democracy that underpin the single-seat electoral system and proportional representation. In addition, they should learn to think critically about the nature of a 'good' Japanese society and relate these principles to the electoral system. They should evaluate the relative merits of the systems in a democratic society.

Outline of sessions

Pre-intervention: Initially, of the 45 students, 14 were for the single-seat electoral district system, 13 were for proportional representation, and 15 were for the system combing these two systems (3 students did not express any preference). They then worked with material that encouraged them to distinguish between facts, claims and values and to structure their arguments to make any conflicts of interest transparent (Ikeno *et al*, 2004).

Introduction: Establishing what students know about the Japanese electoral system

Session 1: Establishing the current facts: a single-seat electoral system combined with proportional representation

Session 2: Analysing the single-seat electoral system with a focus on the electoral system in the UK

- Understanding how the single-seat electoral system operates
- Understanding the interpretations of democracy underpinning the single-seat electoral system
- Considering what this system would mean for Japanese society

Session 3: Analysing proportional representation with a focus on the electoral system in Germany

- Understanding proportional representation
- Understanding the interpretations of democracy behind proportional representation
- Considering what this system would mean for Japanese society

Conclusion

In search of a good society:

- What are the merits of first past the post compared to proportional representation, based on analyses of the UK and German electoral systems?
- Which of these two methods best contributes to the students' notions of a good society?
- Students evaluate the mixed Japanese system.

In this final evaluation, students are asked to demonstrate their knowledge and understanding of how the different systems work, in light of their expectations of a good society. They then come to a judgment about the mixed Japanese electoral system, drawing together their empirical knowledge, and the intentions and social effects of the mixed system.

The structure of individual sessions

Each electoral system is addressed systematically using the Toulmin model described above.

The single-seat electoral system

Data	The facts: one person, one vote; first past the post.
Claim	Good democratic society: alternating parties in power; shifts in power occur peacefully
Warrant	Principles: radical social change possible; the new government may reverse previous policies leading to radical social change. In principle, at least half the nation supports new government.
Backing	Exemplar society and its effects: Thatcher government in UK

Proportional representation

Data	The facts: transferable votes; parties represented in proportion to their strength across the whole country
Claim	Ensures democracy: respects and represents minority opinions
Warrant	Principles: adoption of opposing policies in the coalition cabinet: main party of government might oppose a policy, but if minority-party partner is in favour, policy might be adopted to maintain the coalition cabinet. However, in principle, majority of the nation may oppose the policy
Backing	Exemplar society and its effects: German SPD government in 1998.

Four stages of students' understanding, as evaluated by the teacher

Two questionnaires were administered – one at mid-point and the other at the end. The surveys were analysed with reference to four stages of understanding and judgment:

Stage 1: student shows no understanding of the electoral system

Stage 2: student makes judgments based on some knowledge of the electoral system

> Stage 3: student makes objective judgments based on their knowledge of the electoral system and understanding of its underlying principles
>
> Stage 4: student makes subjective judgments based on their knowledge of the electoral system, taking account of multiple perspectives, understanding of the principles and the notion of 'good democratic society' underlying the system.

The 43 students' preferences did not change significantly between the mid-point and post-discussion surveys: 15 were for the single-seat electoral district system, 11 were for proportional representation, and 16 were for the system using these systems together (1 student abstained).

This is not the place to provide a detailed report. However, according to our analyses of the pre-, mid- and post-project questionnaires, 60 per cent of the students progressed from lower stages to higher stages of reasoning and understanding and 37 per cent did not change. The latter group was already at the higher stages. Three examples follow:

Student U, aged 15, moved from supporting a combined system to proportional representation: 'We could not call it democracy, if the people of each nation are not well informed about their country and its systems.'

Student S, aged 15, initially did not express an opinion, but ultimately supported proportional representation. 'There are many dead votes in the single-seat electoral system and in a system combining these systems.'

Student O, aged 15, maintained and justified his preference for first past the post: 'No government is possible with proportional representation.'

Conclusion

The results of this project offer some insights into students' learning and understanding about controversial issues using the approaches outlined above. These Japanese students had clear views and would like to see changes in the current electoral system. By the end of the project, the majority supported first past the post and were against proportional representation. Most of them developed their critical thinking, knowledge and understanding and their ability to make objective judgements, but had more difficulty with incorporating multiple perspectives. This suggests that students need more support in learning how to take account of multiple perspectives. If this is true then a much-enhanced civics education is of great importance – revealing a gap which needs to be filled in the Japanese education system.

References

Habermas, J. (1981) *Theorie des kommunikativen Handelns*. DK: Ålborg universitets-forlag

Ikeno, N., Watanabe, T. and Takenaka, N. (2004) A study on the Development of Junior High School Civics Courses: Unit-Plan, Considering the democratic society on the basis of election systems, *The Journal of Social Studies,* 91, pp1-11 (in Japanese)

Kato, H. (2003) *Electoral systems in Japan*. Chuokouronsha (in Japanese)

Popper, K. (1987) Zur Theorie der Demokratie, *Der Spiegel,* 41 (32), pp54-55

Toulmin, S. E. (2003) *The Uses of Argument*. Cambridge: Cambridge University Press

Wood for what? Tourism and sustainable development

Ruth Versfeld

Ruth Versfeld asked her secondary age pupils in the Western Cape, South Africa, to engage with a major dilemma in the contemporary world – do ecological imperatives trump the need for people living in poverty to make a living? In this case study she describes in detail how her pupils approached this question – a model which could be used in a variety of contexts with any controversial issue.

This case study is based on an activity I developed with Grade 9 learners (aged 14 to 15) in South African schools. The curriculum was completely overhauled when a democratic government came to power in 1994. This curriculum has since been revised and now takes a strictly outcomes based approach: the 'knowledge focus' or content is specified in order to develop values and competences or measurable skills.

Everyone studies Social Sciences up to Grade 9. This is an optional exit point from a more formally structured education, marking the end of the General Education and Training Phase. The Grade 9 Geography portion of the Social Sciences curriculum is divided into four main sections: Development issues; Sustainable use of resources; Social and environmental conflicts in South Africa, and Mapwork. This points to a strong emphasis on exploring and making informed decisions about social and environmental issues.

'Wood for What?' is an activity that aims to have learners identifying solutions in a situation of conflict. The scenario outlined is realistic in a country where there is considerable rural and urban poverty, where environmental degradation is sometimes horrific and where tourism is a growing and thriving industry.

Part 1: Introductory discussion

A. Read and discuss the short paragraph below:

Conflict is a fact of life. We can't avoid it. What we do have is some control over how we go about finding solutions. The best solutions are where everyone feels that they have gained something. These can be called 'win-win' solutions.

B. Now discuss the ideas in the following paragraph:

Entrepreneurship is a widely encouraged and supported practice in a country where there is considerable unemployment and poverty. People find multiple ways of developing and using skills that others need and can pay for. Tourism brings thousands of people with money into contact with some previously disadvantaged communities. The craft market is a popular attraction. Crafts sold bring much needed money into local communities. Refugees from other parts of Africa often bring fabrics, wooden carvings and other wonderful works from their own countries. These add to the variety and attraction of these markets.

C. Look at this drawing and read the caption.

Many craft items use resources from the natural environment. This drawing shows some of the hardwood animals that can be found in many markets. Deforestation is a local and global problem.

Part 2: Trees or tourists?

There are a number of ways of looking at the scene in this picture. These include:

A. Local African inhabitants in this area were once very poor. However, the growth of the tourist trade has led to these busy markets and a healthy community.

B. Tourists like to spend their dollars at this market. By buying here they are supporting the local economy. Displaying art works such as these in foreign countries helps others to appreciate the talent and expertise of arts and crafts workers in this part of Africa.

C. Huge numbers of slow growing, indigenous trees are chopped down and carved into souvenirs for the tourist market. This practice is not sustainable. The area is becoming deforested. The local community will soon be left with poor soils, flooding, no source of wood and an area that no longer attracts visitors.

Work in groups of three:

1. Read A, B and C above and draw three think bubbles with enough space to write a sentence or two in each.

2. In each think bubble fill in what each of the following groups could be thinking as they look at the picture:

    the wood carvers

    the tourists

    the environmentalists

3. In your group, discuss the issue of selling objects carved from hardwoods. Use this table to organise your ideas:

	Factors affecting the selling of objects made from hardwoods
Economic	
Human rights	
Social	
Environmental	
Other	

4. Read your points to the other groups. Add more to your list.

Part 3: Solving the problem

When I first trialled this part of the activity I asked students to suggest different solutions and to write these into empty speech bubbles. Many found this difficult to do cold. I found it best to introduce some ideas to start the thinking and then to encourage them to add their own. Your class may not be able to generate their own win-win solution at this stage. You could start with a general brainstorm and then add the solutions suggested below.

1. In your groups read this conversation:

   - I think wood carvers should use fast growing trees from the plantations – like pine and gum. It's softer and easier to carve than the hardwoods from the natural forests. They can polish it or dye it darker colours so that it looks more like the real thing.

   - What good will that do? Those tree plantations also harm the environment.

   - Be realistic. There will always be plantations. Crafts use very little wood compared to building.

   - I heard about a woman from Kenya. She started a tree planting project where women grew indigenous trees from seeds. They were paid for every tree they grew. This brought money to the communities and the natural forests grew again.

   - Pay people not to cut down the trees. If the government wants to take care of our natural resources and develop tourism, it should pay those who look after the environment.

   - Tourists want to take African art home with them. Couldn't people do craftwork using other things – like beads, wire, rubber or re-cycled tins and plastic?

2. Summarise the solutions given.

3. Discuss other, new solutions in your group. Write down each new idea.

4. As a group, select the best way forward. This could include more than one solution. Make sure you have win-win ideas that meet the needs of the different role-players – the wood carvers, the tourists and the environmentalists. Check your solution against the factors you identified earlier – Social, Economic, Human Rights, Environmental and Other.

   ☐ Have you solved every aspect of the problem?

   ☐ What new conflicts could arise?

5. Explain your solution to another group. Ask each other questions and try to identify any new conflicts that could be created.

This aspect of anticipating new conflicts is important and worth dwelling on. Listen to the groups as they have their discussions and select one or two proposed solutions to discuss as a class. Predicting possible outcomes of an action is an essential component of selecting an action.

On your own:

6. Write a report about the issue presented in these two pages. It should be at least a page long. Divide your report into three sections:

    Part 1: Explain the problem

    Part 2: Highlight the factors that affect the issue

    Part 3: Suggest a solution where you explain or justify your recommendations.

The notion of win-win comes naturally to most South Africans. Voting for a winner or in favour of a particular decision is not popular in most classrooms I am familiar with. Students prefer to talk and negotiate in order to reach consensus or, at least, a common understanding. This way no one is left feeling like an over-ruled minority. Even when the bell rings for break, most will want to stay on and work out an amicable solution for even the most theoretical of issues. I put this reluctance to vote partly down to the African tradition of Ubuntu. Ubuntu comes from the noun stem 'ntu', which refers to the nature of being human. It is a concept that cannot be captured in a single English word. 'Humanity' is perhaps the closest. It is a way of recognising each person's individual rights and dignity. It is about the respect one person has for another. This way of thinking and acting has helped many groups of people in Africa to live together for generations. We feel it in ourselves as a value to be treasured.

Students may tell each other about things they and others they know have made and sold in a market. While no one finds this a problem, the idea of refugees benefiting too, is not always popular. Xenophobia is a major issue in South Africa but is not the focus of this activity. But I do consider it important to talk about it, whenever it is naturally possible, as it provides students with the opportunity to voice their fears in an environment where opposing points of view can be considered calmly and fairly.

Few Grade 9 students have ever considered the tension between environmental degradation and resources used for making things to sell. Most are taken aback and this is the point at which the activity takes off.

By now they will have seen that there are at least three different points of view. There is potential for conflict. How can we find a win-win solution?

Here are three extracts from Part 3 of the reports written by Grade 9 students. They reflect some interesting thinking:

I think it's a brilliant idea to make more things from beads. African bangles and necklaces sell well. Poor people should be given beads so that they can make and sell things. They can also make wire toys like the Zimbabweans. Then they won't need to cut down trees. They can use some of their money to get electricity so they don't take wood for fires.

I don't think small things are really a problem. It's just those big hippos and giraffe that take lots of wood. The tourists should be more responsible and not buy these things. Then people won't make them!

I don't think it is fair to always ask poor people to recycle tins and plastic. This is the junk of the rich people. Wood carving is a real art. We must grow more trees instead of cutting them down for things like golf courses.

PS: We are tired of all these recycling projects we have to do. People should use less!

Acknowledgement: I have written up this case study in a textbook: *Successful Social Sciences, Grade 9*, Oxford University Press, 2006. This is an adaptation of that text.

Part 3 – Whole School values and action

Political learning and controversial issues with children

Alistair Ross

In this chapter Alistair Ross focuses on political education for children between 7 and 14 years of age. He draws on research to show that primary
age children are not only capable of dealing with political issues, but that
they need to address controversial issues in society, paying adequate
attention to political concepts of power, authority, law and order. He
provides clear guidelines about how to achieve this, noting that teachers
need to move beyond 'safe teaching' about structures and processes, the
neutral and the bland. To do this they need wide conceptual understanding, knowledge and the skills to manage participatory debate and
democracy in the classroom itself.

'Political education' is not a term in frequent use today: for many years it has been regarded with suspicion. In much of Eastern Europe it is now associated with the educational policies of the former regimes and seen as akin to indoctrination. In Western Europe and North America, it has been criticised variously as impossible, unnecessary and an interference with the liberties of the individual or family. Political learning is perceived as *being* controversial, and as *being about* the contro-versial. This chapter examines both charges, and argues that children be-tween the ages of 7 and 14 need to be introduced to the controversial. It examines the fitful development of political education in recent decades, and from this builds a practical model of how teachers can use contro-versial issues to develop political understanding.

There are educational and political arguments against political education for young pupils. From an educational perspective, it has been argued that children are incapable of the sort of complex social thinking needed to understand politics. From the political viewpoint, it is asserted that it is impossible to tackle politics in an unbiased, even-handed way and so should not be attempted, and that any political understanding should not be formally transmitted by the educational system, but should properly be absorbed from family, the media and the political institutions themselves. Both these arguments are flawed, and there has been much resurgence of interest in this area, often through forms of rebranding – as civics education, citizenship education, or political literacy.

The development of political education

There was some interest in political education in UK primary education in the late 1960s and early 1970s as part of the political literacy movement of the time. Crick and Porter (1978) proposed that secondary pupils needed to become politically literate – developing the skills to evaluate political discussion and to make informed judgements between alternatives. Crick (1974) argued that his matrix of core concepts encompassed a far better reality of political activity than the sterile learning of structures.

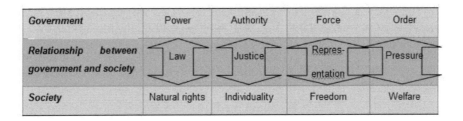

Government	Power	Authority	Force	Order
Relationship between government and society	Law	Justice	Repres-entation	Pressure
Society	Natural rights	Individuality	Freedom	Welfare

These ideas were taken up by some teachers of younger children, and through the 1970s there were primary school developments in political understanding. They included getting children to role-play decision-making about difficult situations on a deserted island, discussions of authority and power in local decisions, and drawing parallels between political and human politics. In this way, some children became skilled at dealing with controversial or disputed subject matter, albeit often through a make-believe world.

The 1980s were, in contrast, a period in which any form of teaching about society, let alone politics, was discouraged. The National Curriculum of 1988 allowed only the most traditional subjects taught in a tightly controlled manner. Rather than foreground the democratic substance of citizenship, the emphasis was on the responsibilities that the citizen owed the state. Political and social education was downgraded as successive Ministers of Education promoted the core subjects, and left no place for learning about how society worked and the inevitable controversies within heterogeneous, multicultural communities (Ahier and Ross, 1994).

Ten years later a review of the National Curriculum and the subsequent Crick report (QCA, 1998) led to the introduction of the new subject of Citizenship, formed around three strands: Social and moral responsibility, Community involvement and Political literacy. Citizenship education is now mandatory in secondary schools, and recommended in primary schools.

There have been parallel moves in the European Union, including initiatives designed to improve the understanding of European political institutions and calls for European citizenship. In *Towards a Europe of Knowledge* the former Commissioner for Education and Youth, Edith Cresson, called for 'the development of a sense of belonging to a common social and cultural area ... a broader-base understanding of citizenship founded on mutual understanding of the cultural diversities that constitute Europe's originality and richness' (European Commission, 1997).

Politicians' arguments for political education

Why have these politicians sought to introduce political education? Why now? And what implications does their model have for how teachers are expected to approach controversial issues in their teaching?

Citizenship education is being initiated in many countries, in the UK and the European Union at a time when there is a real decline in understanding, sympathy and trust in politicians and political institutions. The UK elections of 2001 and 2005 showed declining voter turnout (Electoral Commission, 2005), and the European Parliamentary elections in 1999 had a remarkably low participation rate. Younger voters are even less inclined to turn out to vote than older generations. The traditional explanation for this disinterest is that we have not had sufficient political education (Bromley *et al*, 2004).

Politicians argue that schools have let down the nation: if the schools told the kids about the virtues of democracy, all would be well. Politicians fear that without popular endorsement at the polls, they lack authority: getting people to believe in the systems that they stand for might restore their legitimacy: some call it a 'democratic deficit' (Moravcsik, 2004). Such concern is a powerful motivating force for the current political emphasis on programmes for citizenship. Political education is being introduced, at least in part, to address a political problem and is itself controversial.

The conception of democracy is also controversial. Traditional representative democracy simply ensures intermittent participation in elections, through political parties that stand for broad principles. But there are other kinds of democratic action, and over the past two decades many people have become involved in more specific political activities, rather than supporting political parties. The growth of single issue politics has challenged traditional politicians, who have found electors – and young people in particular – deserting mass parties in favour of pressure groups, such as Drop the Debt, Comic Relief, Make Poverty History and coalitions of Greens (Holden, 2006). The old political parties have had their activities and compromises challenged by informed political activists. This alternative democracy is less concerned with the political structures and procedures than with the issues themselves.

But this is not what politicians and public servants want political education to be about. Their concerns are – quite naturally – with buttressing the systems and institutions that brought them into existence and that maintain them. They are also about civic duties and obligations – to participate in political processes, to understand the need for compromise, to accept the decision-making processes. If future citizens can be told how fair the existing system is, how the machinery of government works in the interest of the citizen, how interest groups must of course be listened to while balancing competing interests – they will then accept the legitimacy of the political processes, and become the good citizen.

Citizenship itself is not without controversy. Citizenship of what territorial unit? Britain, England or the UK? There is a certain irony in the English National Curriculum promoting British Citizenship, where Britain is only a part of the state of the United Kingdom. European citizenship presents further challenges: some people also feel threatened by the erosion of the idea of the nation-state. Those who need the authority of a state, who choose to identify strongly with conceptions of 'their race', their genetic stock, are undermined by questions that challenge the legitimacy of this institution.

Many educators in Europe today have approached the concept of European identity with some caution, suggesting that citizenship based on the new Europe must be distinctly different from the old citizenships of the nation-states: less ethnocentric, more diverse, more inclusive, less wedded to nationalistic conceptions. Osler and Starkey (2003) have built on David Held's (1995) work on cosmopolitan democracy to advocate 'cosmopolitan citizenship', which, they argue, will prepare young people to live together in increasingly diverse local communities and an interdependent world. Hladnik (1995) argues that European citizenship should not be limited as a legal definition of status, and suggests that refugees should also be regarded as citizens, in a broad and inclusive definition, separate from historical definitions of citizenship by birth, ancestry or naturalisation. The European programmes make much of the ideas of nested identities, and seek to promote citizenship at European level as part of a self-identity that includes national and regional elements.

The educational case for political education

This brings the argument back to the contemporary classroom. Primary teachers are increasingly sure that children can understand political issues in a meaningful way, but there has been a dearth of research into this area since the initial groundbreaking studies by Greenstein (1965), Connell (1971) and Coles (1986). In the UK, Stevens suggested that seven year olds 'have some cognitive contact with the political world': they see political power as 'limited, consented to and conditional upon results' (1982:38).

The work of teachers in the 1970s shows how children are able to develop political understanding. Margerison (1972) described an extended project, lasting several months, in which junior children developed an island society which included social and political dimensions. Riches (1974) worked with 10-11 year olds to develop a politically-focussed programme based around the island theme, where links were made between the simulated activities and contemporary political processes. Wagstaff (1978) developed materials that encouraged the systematic examination of eight social/political concepts through three environments that figured significantly in children's lives – the family, friendship groups and work. Ross (1981) used political fables such as Adams' *Watership Down* (1972), and Orwell's *Animal Farm* (1945) to draw parallels with human behaviour. Denscombe and Conway (1982) used issues in development education to help children examine a range of political concepts around a conceptual framework. In all cases, the educators were drawing on children's experiences to identify examples of conflict and its resolution.

This approach has several common characteristics and is relevant for today's classroom. It utilises children's experience – both direct and vicarious – from role-playing, modelling, sharing stories, or watching the news. It uses discussion to get children to articulate their thoughts and actively construct meaning from the experience. By developing ideas in a social context with their peers and with teachers and other adults, a shared understanding is achieved. The experience is around something that is controversial, involving dissent and disagreement.

Issues of social justice (the treatment of suspected terrorism, or of asylum seekers), of environmental change (global warning, conservation, nuclear energy), and of war and peace (Iraq, Palestine, Sri Lanka ...) are put before children every day, and can evoke intense interests and passion. These are 'issues' because they are controversial, and it is *because* they are controversial that they are interesting to children, and *because* they are controversial that it is important that future citizens learn how to understand them and how to take up defendable positions. It could be argued that it is the responsibility of the educational system to ensure that children develop strategies to understand, analyse, make decisions and argue beliefs around such issues, in the same way, and for the same reasons, that schools help children understand fundamental science and learn to read.

These examples demonstrate an interpretation of citizenship which goes much further than learning to vote for politicians who will make decisions, and volunteering to help others in the community. Active citizens make efforts to understand what is going on, and to act on their analyses.

Concept-based approaches
Behind many of the earlier attempts to engage children in the controversial was the idea of a network of broad social concepts that, it was argued, could be used to organise analysis and comparison. Conceptual frameworks for learning were increasingly popular in the 1970s: Bruner's work in the MACOS project and Senesh's programme *Our Working World* illustrated how social, political and economic concepts could be developed in children. They built up concepts through repeated exposure to case studies, through strategies which encouraged classroom discussion so that meanings could be jointly constructed and made relevant to pupils' experiences (Bruner and Haste, 1987).

One problem of this approach is that it can lead to over-emphasising the issues or the experiential element of the learning. It is possible to develop an approach through a whole series of important social and political issues – engaging to the children, focused on experiences, arousing concern – which are not harnessed to any underlying conceptual structures or frameworks. A teacher can develop lively classroom topics on environmental issues, but if there is no an attempt to encourage reflection on the principles of political behaviour that lie behind them, a valuable educational experience is lost. Children need to construct a view of adult behaviour that enables them to see competing interests, power structures, systems of law construction and of justice and authority systems that underpin how these issues are dealt with. This contrasts starkly with a primary ideology where teachers may present complex social issues in terms of simple solutions, with clearly defined 'good' and 'bad' perspectives. Thus Steiner (1992), evaluating how teachers approach world studies, concluded that

> Most teachers concentrate on the self-esteem building, interpersonal and cooperative element of the world studies approach. They also engage in work that questions stereotypes such as racism or sexism. The environment, local or 'rain forest', is a common theme. Global issues, such as those to do with the injustice inherent in the current systems of the global economy, or highlighting the cultural achievements and self-sufficiency of Southern societies ... receive far less attention. (1992:9)

Teachers can also be tempted to take short-cuts, or to mistake the outcome for the process by offering children ready-made definitions or summaries that become the 'correct' answer. For example, guidelines for primary teachers in social studies produced in 1980 offered definitions such as

> *Power* is the ability to make others do as you want them to. *Authority* is based on the respect and obedience given to someone because of some official post that they hold and because they are agreed to have some personal ability and excellence in the task. (ILEA, 1980:7)

Given such definitions, it is all too easy to teach these summaries directly to children, rather than helping children to construct their meaning through repeated exposure to examples and discussion of them. This approach leads to a model of transmitting accepted knowledge which assumes that when one has the facts, one can begin to understand political activity. This kind of political education confirms the legitimacy of politicians, and the justice and the equity that they promote. It reinforces the uncontroversial and bland.

The trouble is that the pupils know better: they are aware that despite its rhetoric, the system isn't handling a whole range of social, political and economic issues that concern them – racism, poverty, the environment, housing, pollution, corruption. Children do have such concerns, as evidenced, for example, in Claire (2001), which articulates the clear and often strong views children hold about the world around them – about family and the politics of family life, about gender and sex, identity and racism, economic and social inequality. If one wants to engage children in a learning process about politics, one has to start with such issues.

A model for classroom action

The solution is a delicate balance combining several elements: experiences, issues, concepts and structures and processes. All are necessary components – no single one may be left out. The sequence of the learning programme is also critical. Crick's (1974) conceptual model, given at the beginning of this chapter, is as good as any, but this might be supplemented by the ILEA list of social studies concepts: power and authority, the division of labour, social control, conflict, interdependence, cooperation, tradition and social change (ILEA: 1980).

Stage one: begin with issues firmly grounded in the pupils' own experience. Select issues that are known – or can be predicted – to provoke some differences in the class. This will depend, particularly with young children, on the location and composition of the community in which the school is set – rural, urban, multicultural, and so on. Working in primary school classrooms as a class teacher in the 1980s, it was clear to me that the way to engage children in political education was to get them to talk, discuss and argue about controversial issues. It wasn't to talk about structures: it was to get them to take on particular matters of concern: controversial issues, such as poverty, homelessness, pollution, capitalism, gender, ethnicity and language all invited discussion. The role of the teacher is to facilitate argument, to protect different points of view, and to be prepared to challenge the children's viewpoints. I would put forward my own views, insisting that they were mine and need not be theirs.

An example: migration to the UK from Eastern Europe.
Raising a topical issue such as this might let loose a range of opinions and comment, possibly partly based on headlines in the popular press. An initial discussion might be rather lop-sided, with views expressed about 'our country', a 'crowded island', 'scroungers', 'living on benefits', 'taking our jobs', 'bringing diseases', and so on. There may also be views about an aging population, the need for workers, freedom of movement, and so on. At this stage, the teacher's role would be

- *to protect the views of minorities in the class – whose presence might in any case meliorate extreme views*
- *to help sort out the issues being raised, perhaps gently pointing to the inconsistencies between 'living on benefits' and 'taking our jobs'*
- *suggesting where, how and what further information the class might seek.*

Stage two: the teacher plans out a programme, mapping the events and processes that surround the issue on a conceptual map. Crick's conceptual framework could be useful, to check that debates and arguments include some core ideas of politics – rule of law, representation, democracy, political rights, separation of powers, and more – and to ensure that discussion draws on these ideas and helps form an understanding of what these concepts are. Issue-based teaching needs a conceptual framework at its core, and in the mind of the teacher, if it is to amount to political education.

How do the issues raised in our example match Crick's grid of concepts?

An initial check (overleaf) suggests that most of these fall in the 'societal' row, and that after discussion and illumination of each item, these might then be taken back, through the 'relationships' row, to issues of government. For example children can investigate the rights of migrants and indigenes and the relationship between these and our system of laws, to understand where power lies.

Stage three: the teacher needs to engage in discussion: to be provocative, to be a chair who permits dissent, who puts forward views – while maintaining that it is only a view – who protects minorities, encourages the more reticent and advocates alternative positions. The teacher's role is not neutral – we do not want children to be neutral on issues they are passionate about. The intention is to give the class a model for engaging in political argument, of passing on by example the values of political debate – listening to others, putting forward evidence and arguments, allowing people to differ, picking up and elaborating points of similarity and difference. This includes putting cases that challenge the children's views – if necessary making it clear that they are not your views – in a way that allows the class to respond, to rebut, and to challenge them. This is particularly important if there is unanimity in the class: they need to know that others may have different views, and they need to rehearse their arguments against them.

Government	Power	Authority	Force	Order
Relationship between government and society	Law *What rights do fellow citizens of the EU have? What UK laws might over-ride these rights – at least, in the short run?*	Justice	Representation	Pressure
Society	Natural rights *The right to work and travel within Europe? The right to maintain a cultural identity?*	Individuality *What rights do individuals have, as opposed to groups?*	Freedom *What balances might there be between the freedom of an economic migrant to better themselves and the freedom of UK citizens to reject them?*	Welfare *What pressures are put on our welfare services by migrants? What contribution do migrants make to paying for, and staffing, these services?*

This is a challenging position for the teacher. For example, I once chaired a passionate discussion with a group of nine year olds who were incensed that some south-east Asian countries ate dogs, and unanimous in their disapproval: I found myself in the position of arguing for cultural tolerance and the right of people in other countries to make their own decisions on culinary rules and preferences. I didn't persuade a single child, and was the subject of occasional strange looks from children in the school for several months.

- ■ *If the class are unanimous about migrants, challenge their views with alternative viewpoints:*
    - – get them to justify what they say
    - – offer counter-examples, information about the low level of take-up of benefits, for example, or about migrants taking jobs others won't take, or creating new wealth for us all.

■ *Offer a model of how to argue a case:*
  - show them how to avoid pejorative and offensive language (as well as telling them why it's offensive)
  - demonstrate how to make a series of points
  - show them how to construct a sequenced argument.

■ *If the class is divided, encourage exploration of each issue from different perspectives*
  - don't reduce the issue to 'for' and 'against'
  - encourage a multiplicity of views.

Stage four: encourage the class to find out information about alternatives, about facts. This stage is a return to more traditional teaching: it may involve reference sources and library work but also interviewing people, conducting surveys, talking with parents and with other adults, or visiting particular locations. Meanwhile, the teacher must check the conceptual map. After the initial discussions, does it appear that additional concepts are going to be raised? Will the concepts in the original list all be present?

■ *Collect material with the class*
  - in a topical case like this, much will be from the press and the internet.
  - you might also be able to invite an economic migrant into the class, to talk about their life, journey and work.

■ *Does the conceptual map still work*
  - are all the 'society' concepts being explored?
  - how far are discussions being moved towards concepts which relate to government?

Stage five: re-engage in debate, bringing in the new knowledge the children have researched, and encourage reflection, comparison, alternatives that can be used to encourage the drawing out of generalisations. Conceptual learning slowly becomes evident. When a child begins to draw two events together, and can point to similarities in them, analyse the commonalities and begin to make a prediction, a rule that might apply – this is when the concept begins. Encourage it. It may well be only partly formed; it may well be wrong in terms of adult definition. You don't have to agree with it, but praise the way of thinking, and endorse the process. Saying 'No, that's not right' because you've not thought of x or y will stop further efforts to generalise. With a bit of luck, another child will raise fresh evidence that challenges the generalisation. Consider what other information might lead to a refinement of the concept. The principle is to get the child that put the proposition forward to rethink it, and to accommodate new material in a reformulation.

- *Can the class talk about their ideas in terms of conflicting rights, about welfare, freedoms and individuals?*
- *Do they illustrate these ideas with examples from the discussion and their research? Are ideas changing, or being modified, or becoming more subtly nuanced?*
- *Does any of the evidence that has been collected challenge the initial ideas?*

Stage six: the teacher will need to provide the structural information about the processes, procedures and forms of the political system that will enlighten and supplement the class's understanding. Voting procedures, the role of MPs, the Government and the police, the place of law: all this will now – and probably only now – be of interest and relevance. The machinery is much more interesting, and better understood, when children know what they want to do with it.

Having completed this round, start again. But this time take a new issue, that will pick up on some different concepts with the objective of visiting, over the year or years, all the major concepts. And always encourage reflection and comparison, re-evaluation.

This is challenging. Teachers need a broad understanding of how structures work, a conceptual framework on to which they can map issues as they arise, and to maintain a pedagogic style that permits them not to know the answers, and to not be the authority. To get away from safe teaching about structures and processes, about the neutral and the bland, we need to ensure that teachers are equipped with wide conceptual understanding, with knowledge of the issues that might illustrate these, and with the skills to manage covering the issues of participatory democracy through handling political debate in the classroom. Much work is to be done in developing these skills.

References

Adams, R (1972) *Watership Down*. London: Collins (Penguin/Puffin, 1973)

Ahier, J. and Ross, A. (1994) (eds) *The Social Subjects in the Curriculum*. London: Falmer

Bromley, C., Curtice, J. and Seyd, B. (2004) Is Britain Facing a Crisis of Democracy? *Centre for Research into Elections and Social Trends,* Working paper http://www.crest.ox.ac.uk/papers/p106.pd

Bruner, J. and Haste, H. (eds) (1987) *Making Sense: The Child's Construction of the World*. London: Methuen

Claire, H. (2001) *Not Aliens: primary school children and the Citizenship/PSHE curriculum*. Stoke-on-Trent: Trentham Books

Coles, R. (1986) *The Political Life of Children*. Boston: Atlantic Monthly Press

Connell R. W. (1971) *The Child's Construction of Politics*. Melbourne: Melbourne University Press

Crick, B. (1974) Basic Political Concepts and Curriculum Development, *Teaching Politics*, 3,1

Crick, B. and Porter, A. (1978) *Political education and political literacy*. London: Longman for the Hansard Society

Denscombe, M. and Conway, L. (1982) Autonomy and Control in Curriculum Innovation: A Case study of Development Education in the Primary School, *Teaching Politics*, 11,3

Electoral Commission (2005) Election 2005 Turnout: *How Many, Who and Why?* http://www.electoralcommission.org.uk/files/dms/Election2005turnoutFINAL_18826-13874__E__N__S__W__.pdf

European Commission (1997) *Towards a Europe of Knowledge*: Com (97 (563), Brussels: European Commission

Greenstein, F. (1965) *Children and Politics*. Yale: Yale University Press

Held, D. (1995) *Democracy and the Global Order. From the Modern State to Cosmopolitan Governance*. Cambridge: Polity Press

Hladnik, M. (1995) All Different – All Equal: who defines education for citizenship in a new Europe?' in Osler, A., Rathenow, H-F. and Starkey, H. (eds) *Teaching for Citizenship in Education*, Stoke-on-Trent: Trentham Books

Holden, C. (2006) Concerned citizens: children and the future, Education, *Citizenship and Social Justice*, 1 (3), pp231-247

Inner London Education Authority (1980) *Social Studies in the Primary School (ILEA Curriculum Guidelines)*, London: ILEA Learning Materials Service

Margerison, C. (1972) A learning experiment in social studies education: aspects of children's political understanding and development, *Teaching Politics*, 1 (1)

Moravcsik, A. (2004) Is there a 'Democratic Deficit' in World Politics? A Framework for Analysis, *Government and Opposition*, 39 (2), p336

Orwell, G. (1945) *Animal Farm*. London: Secker and Warburg (Penguin, 1951)

Osler, A. and Starkey, H. (2003) Learning for cosmopolitan citizenship: theoretical debates and young people's experiences, *Educational Review*, 55 (3), pp243-254

QCA (1998) *Education for citizenship and the teaching of democracy in schools: Final report of the advisory group on citizenship*. London: Qualifications and Curriculum Authority

Riches, J. (1974) Education for Democracy: A curriculum unit for Upper Juniors, *Teaching Politics* 3, 2 (and second part, 3, 3)

Ross A. (1981) Using literature to develop political concepts in the primary school, *Teaching Politics*, 10 (1)

Steiner, M. (1992) *World Studies 8-13: evaluating active learning*. Manchester: Manchester Metropolitan University, World Studies Trust

Stevens, O. (1982) *Children Talking Politics: Political Learning in Childhood*. Oxford: Martin Robertson

Wagstaff, S. (1978) *Teacher's Guide: People Around Us – 1: Families*. London: Inner London Education Authority

Taking risks, building peace: teaching conflict strategies and skills to students aged 6 to 16+

Kathy Bickmore

In this chapter Kathy Bickmore points out that there are constructive as well as destructive ways to handle conflict but that positive peace building strategies need to be taught and learned. She describes a variety of practical approaches which have been implemented successfully with pupils of different ages in Canadian schools.

Research with young boys and girls indicates that gains in peaceful conflict resolution are indeed possible, most notably with young boys. Moreover, typically female approaches to conflict can enrich democratic resolution of controversy.

Human life revolves around conflicts – disagreements, problems, decisions, clashing perspectives or interests – personal, local and global. Violence can be a symptom of underlying conflicts, or a way of handling conflicts, but it is not inevitable. The nonviolent confrontation, management and eventual resolution of such conflicts is what sustains democratic civil society and intergroup and interpersonal relationships. Like oxygen, conflict can be explosive – but it is inescapable and essential to life.

Conflict itself is no barrier to peace: it can be handled constructively or destructively. 'Negative peace,' meaning *absence* of overt violence, is a valuable partial goal (Galtung, 1996). The more complex goal of 'positive peace' focuses on the *presence* of justice and of mechanisms for on-going problem-solving. Democratic processes are mechanisms for managing conflict nonviolently- for example, to protect rights in social relationships, to regulate the development and exchange of resources to meet human needs, and to engage in critical reasoning to make collective decisions for problem-solving. Thus democratisation and peace building are inter-twined, in global life and in classroom learning.

Where conflict situations are escalated, intense and harmful, coercive *peacekeeping* – security control or intervention to restore negative peace – is more necessary, while pro-active peace building – dialogue and restora-tive problem-solving to create positive peace and prevent future harm – becomes more difficult (Bickmore, 2004). Thus *education* would have to take risks to build peace. Continual, pro-active, constructive engagement with conflict may develop individuals' and communities' capacity for positive peace, *before* the next emergency occurs. This chapter, describes the ingredients of conflict and conflict management learning that can offer a solid foundation for teaching about intense conflicts and contro-versy.

Learning peace building: incorporating conflict in the curriculum

Nonviolence, like violence, is *learned* behaviour. A student's or teacher's repertoire of skills for handling conflict, and their confidence in applying those skills, improve with elaboration and practice. A curriculum for posi-tive peace and democratic citizenship, therefore, would give all youngsters opportunities to practise handling taboo topics and unsettling viewpoints (conflict), by investigating the complex social and political issues that are more difficult to learn, or would be learned in adversarial ways, in homes and neighbourhoods (Merelman, 1990). Education for peace building in-cludes:

- ▪ explicit *teaching* about conflict and peace, for understanding and skill development
- ▪ implicit modeling and practice through *peacemaking interven-tion*
- ▪ *equity initiatives* to nurture resilient and inclusive relationships and climates.

Conflict education has implications for both nonviolent behaviour and academic learning. For example, a conflict mediation program imple-mented in several inner-city elementary schools included all the above educational elements: conflict resolution training for age 8 to 11 peer mediators who in turn led learning activities for their peers; mediation of student disputes by the trained peer mediators, and attention to equity and inclusivity in selecting and supporting the mediators. After a year of implementation, the average 8 to 11-year-old boy's conflict management skills and inclinations, measured by a pre/ post survey, had improved even more than their average female classmates', whose verbal skills and inclinations to use nonviolence had started out higher (Bickmore, 2002b).

Such peace building initiatives can strengthen academic proficiency by resolving obstacles to attendance and on-task engagement, and also by teaching academically-relevant skills such as communication and problem-solving. At the same time, academic curricula that address conflict constructively can provide opportunities to apply, practise and discuss peace building concepts and skills. Peace building education is implemented, and the use of punitive approaches to peacekeeping, such as suspension from school, may be reduced by reducing the incidence of aggressive behaviour as well as providing adults with alternative responses to certain conflicts.

News media and popular culture remind us that people find conflict – social and interpersonal – fascinating. In the postmodern context, even very young children are aware of difficult conflicts and violence in the world, whether or not their parents and teachers discuss these problems openly. Students, especially marginalised students such as ethnocultural minorities and working class girls, may consider classroom knowledge implausible, irrelevant or boring when it ignores the conflicts and viewpoints they see and live. Katherine Simon (2001) argues that moral and existential questions are too often avoided or barely discussed in many classrooms, even though, when they are, students generally consider such discussions their most important learning experiences. Indeed, many young people become more engaged in classroom learning, and interested in politically-relevant subject-matter, when their divergent viewpoints are discussed and respected (Torney-Purta *et al*, 2001).

Conflict learning is bound up in matters of gender identity. Although there are important variations across cultures, femininity is stereotypically associated with nurturing, passive or collaborative responses to conflict. Masculinity is stereotypically associated with defensive, aggressive or competitive responses to conflict. Children learn about how they are expected to manage social and interpersonal conflicts, along with their development as 'good' girls and boys. Thus feminist perspectives can illuminate and help to remediate the anti-democratic aspects of what sometimes passes for citizenship or conflict resolution education.

People can make citizenship choices only to the extent that they know about alternatives to mainstream, normalised information and roles (Vibert and Shields, 2003). For example, the predominant narrative in history represents only a small proportion of even the male population – heroes, white dominant-class leaders of government and military actions in Northern colonial powers with the occasional heroic exception. Female and visible minority roles that really reflect alternative viewpoints – for example in labour and human rights movements, building communities, working for peace – are still not prominent in mainstream and mandated curriculum materials, at least in North America. However, it is not merely a matter of *adding* information about marginalised people and human rights violations, as if the basic story were the same. Kevin Kumashiro argues that anti-oppressive teaching should challenge the partial and biased nature of both curriculum resources and students' prior knowledge (2004). Raising questions about the hidden stories underlying political and historical phenomena can disrupt 'the repetition of comforting knowledges' (p 47), and provoke desire for further learning.

Curriculum is more than subject-matter: people learn from what they experience and practise, including who speaks in class, and who is heard. For example, girls who are non-disruptive are often ignored (Sadker *et al*, 1991), while girls who resist aggressively, as well as lower-status and visible minority youth, may be sanctioned more harshly than other students who act in similar ways (Slee, 1995). Given students' different status and experiences, conflict learning depends on the creation of both sufficient safety and sufficient challenge for diverse participants. Safer learning climates encourage openness to wider margins of respected viewpoints, initiate thoughtful analysis of the inevitable discontinuities in democratic life and taking responsibility to confront bigotry and hurtful behaviour when it does occur. Trusting relationships and strong communities stem not from a lack of conflict but from opportunities to confront and repair the inevitable disjunctures.

Developing confidence for managing conflict

Many teachers feel inadequately prepared to address meaningful peace building citizenship questions and controversies in the classroom (Wilson *et al*, 2002). Subject-matter preparation does matter: teachers do not always notice gaps or misleading information, topics or language for questioning. Their awareness of where to find alternatives, and why, is a precondition for students to develop such capacities in the classroom. At the same time, *quantity* of knowledge cannot substitute for *quality* of knowledge, nor for confidence in engaging with that knowledge. One way to develop teachers' capacities for handling conflict and controversy is to encourage consultation, dissent and dialogue among peers (Bickmore, 2005b). As Simon points out, 'controversy is inevitable when people talk about things that matter to them' and curriculum always has moral ramifications that are not – and should not be – neutral (2001:219). Cultures of enquiry, transparency and dialogue among staff can help schools to address such conflicts constructively. Thus controversy can serve as a motivation and frame for teacher development, just as it can for children's curriculum.

It is impossible to practise conflict resolution or peace building without addressing conflict. However, one can build safety and confidence by beginning with relatively simple conflict concepts, communication skills and paths toward resolution, before addressing more difficult controversial public issues and intense conflicts. A sequence like the following can ground conflict/peace building learning in a coherent conceptual framework and sequential skill development:

- understanding conflict: actions, eg violence, vs problems, incompatible wants and needs
- communicating about conflict: talking and listening, expressing feelings, questioning, perspectives and perceptions
- responding to conflict: options, interests, and consequences
- conflict resolution processes: negotiation, mediation, peacemaking circles
- complex conflict cases near and far: infusion of meaningful conflicts in curriculum

Below, I illustrate some ways to teach these key concepts. They can be addressed in developmentally appropriate ways with a wide variety of learners, children and adults.

Understanding conflict

The experience of conflict is familiar to everyone, at least from the time a very young child learns to say 'no!' However, the concepts and vocabulary for understanding conflict and the options it presents, for distinguishing the underlying problems from their symptoms or behaviours such as violence, are more elusive. Making implicit cultural knowledge explicit, for example through role playing and discussion, can empower learners to re-think and build upon that knowledge (Lederach, 1995).

A basic concept development approach was used in an elementary (age 9 to 11) classroom with diverse language-minority pupils (Bickmore, 1999). The teacher invited them to brainstorm examples of conflicts they had witnessed or participated in, prompting for problems and disagreements the children had encountered at different points in the day with different people, such as disagreeing with their mother about when to get out of bed or what to eat for breakfast, and disputes with siblings. Later, the class diversified their list of examples by identifying conflicts in stories they had read, such as settler vs. aboriginal control of land in a book about pioneers, and in the news, such as a then-current series of workers' union protests against the provincial government. The children worked together to distinguish what were examples of conflict, and then to name what the examples had in common. In my teacher education course, we also cate-gorise the examples of conflict into types.

The teacher guided the students to examine the sources and triggers of conflict – what people disagreed or competed about – focusing on human needs and wants, and the idea that participants see problems from dif-ferent perspectives. For example, children were invited to share their own responses to the question, 'what bothers you or makes you angry?' When invited to draw pictures depicting conflicts over needs, it was interesting that the children chose tangible needs that often involve political de-cisions, such as access to unpolluted water, food, housing or health care funding.

Much later in the unit, most of these children were able to discuss in-tangible personal needs and desires such as friendship, respect or inclu-sion, in relation to the interpersonal but complex problem of bullying in their own playground. This demonstrates the value of anchoring conflict learning in key concepts, rather than confusing symptoms or aggressive actions with the underlying conflicts themselves, or assuming that local interpersonal conflicts are more comprehensible than global social con-flicts.

Communicating about conflict

The ability to communicate effectively is a basic goal of education, espe-cially in the language arts and health education. Articulating points of view orally and in writing, tailoring persuasion to different audiences, effective listening, summarising and interpreting unfamiliar information and viewpoints, recognising bias and constructive criticism are among many literacy and information skills common to both conflict management and academic proficiency. For example, grade 4-6 English Language Arts curriculum expectations in Nova Scotia, Canada emphasise critical literacy, such as recognising 'how text constructs one's understanding and worldview of race, gender, social class, age, ethnicity and ability' (Bickmore, 2005a). High school English expectations in Manitoba, Canada include visual media representations as well as written text such as 'students need to recognise that what a camera captures is a construction of reality, not reality itself' (*ibid*). Children aged 6 to 8 can be guided to discern who is telling the story read aloud to them and to imagine how it might be different if another character told the story; older children can act as television interviewers to enact, detect, and stimulate reflection upon bias in news media representations (TDSB, 2003).

Conflict resolution activities often practise inclusive communication through circle sharing, offering all participants clear opportunities to participate – or pass – such as asking 'how did you feel [in a conflict] when...' Secondary students may practise a complex listening exercise developed by Peter Elbow, called the Believing Game (Hargreaves, 1997). In this, each student writes down between 10 and 20 reasons for their own viewpoint on a particular issue, then listens carefully while somebody presents to the class an unpopular view on that issue, role-played or real. Listeners are invited to ask the speaker questions that could help them to understand elements of the contrary viewpoint, such as 'what experiences have led you to this opinion?' During the activity, listeners are asked to temporarily silence their internal 'buts' and doubts, and to verbally affirm any elements of the speaker's opinion that they are able to 'believe.' In debriefing, students first paraphrase the unpopular viewpoint and describe whether and how their own viewpoints might have changed during the process. Lastly, students review their lists of reasons for their initial viewpoints, modify and strengthen them based on what they have learned, and articulate their remaining disagreements with the opposing viewpoint. This exercise affirms the value of dissenting views, practises open-ended questioning, and distinguishes listening from agreeing or doing what another prefers.

Responding to conflict

Conflict presents choices. Conflicts embody different possibilities and viewpoints about what can or should be done and people can respond in a range of ways. It is crucial to distinguish avoidance responses from those dealing with a problem. This is especially important in preparing people to address challenging controversies. Sometimes avoiding or postponing confrontation is a sensible response to a particular situation, to ensure safety: however by themselves, accommodation or violence cannot lead to actual resolution of the conflicts, nor transformation of fractured relationships. Resolution requires distinguishing the person to blame, from the problem of what each actually needs and wants. It is more useful to expand children's experience and teach various assertive approaches, than to confront or de-escalate conflict.

A good place to start is to ask people to imagine how they would respond to a hypothetical scenario. With an older group, for example, imagine somebody with whom you have a conflict is coming down the hallway toward you; or with younger children, imagine that somebody spilled tomato ketchup on your favourite shirt. After participants share their range of responses, these can be categorised as fight (violence), flight (avoidance) or alternatives (assertive nonviolent options).

Two aspects of responses to conflict are especially important: creative thinking to imagine and invent a wide range of options for handling the problem, and then critical thinking to assess those options and predict their consequences, in light of the desires and needs or interests of each stakeholder. The influential negotiation book *Getting to Yes* (Fisher *et al*, 1991) emphasises the importance of 'inventing before deciding' to create powerful options that may help satisfy the interests of each side, in order to resolve the problem.

There is no reason to limit practice scenarios to the interpersonal level. Sometimes distant conflicts over tangible interests are easier to view in their broad outlines than are conflicts at home in which pupils are directly implicated. For example, the elementary curriculum unit described above (Bickmore, 1999) took place during the aftermath of the 1994 Rwandan genocidal clash. Inspired by a news story about Hutu refugees returning to find an otherwise-homeless Tutsi family living in what had been their house, the teacher assembled children in two equal lines facing one another, representing Tutsi and Hutu family members, and they acted out, with no physical contact, what they might have done in such a situation.

Group role play strategies like this tend to decrease individuals' shyness about trying out unfamiliar actions.

Later, children shared their various responses and brainstormed additional options for handling this conflict. They categorised each option as win-win (both parties' wants and needs met), win-lose (one party's needs met at the expense of the other), or lose-lose (the housing problem unresolved from both perspectives). In their sometimes-passionate arguments with peers about which consequences they predicted for each response to this conflict, the children practised prediction and reasoning about choices that could escalate, de-escalate, or resolve conflicts. Later, they applied these insights to their own context by interviewing someone in their family or community about responses to current protests against the provincial government.

Identifying each stakeholder's interests in a conflict takes practice. This can be applied to a wide range of conflicts. In my teacher education course, participants invent and later assess in relation to their values and needs, responses to a typical collegial conflict over use of shared classroom or office space, and practise questioning to identify the interests underlying adversarial or attacking statements. Because creative thinking is often the most neglected element of conflict resolution, they also practise brainstorming options in more amusing contexts, for example imagining alternative uses for a common object.

Conflict resolution processes
These three elements of conflict education form a solid foundation for addressing controversial social and political issues, and can be adapted to diverse contexts. But what of processes for constructively and effectively resolving conflict? Learning contrasting processes makes visible the choices embodied in each, thus helping participants to develop culturally and contextually appropriate conflict management strategies.

Probably the most well-known conflict resolution processes are the standard consultative meeting format known as parliamentary procedure, typically involving a chairperson, speakers representing various viewpoints and proposals, and decision-making by majority vote, and the judicial format, typically involving a judge or tribunal, lawyers and fact-finders representing two opposing viewpoints, and decision-making, assigning blame via arbitration. Both these approaches are commonly reflected in simulation activities designed for classroom learning (USIP,

2005). Two other less well known approaches are also applicable to conflict learning and deliberation on controversial issues: these are mediation and peacemaking circle processes and are drawn from community conflict resolution.

Mediation is voluntary negotiation between conflicting parties, or representatives, with the aid of a third-party facilitator or mediator, who is not a decision-maker on the content of the dispute but a guide for the dialogue process. Various approaches to mediation are also applicable to direct negotiation without a mediator – when a third-party facilitates some safe and constructive negotiations, participants develop skills and relationships that may allow them to negotiate more of their conflicts autonomously (Harris, 2005). The novice mediator role can be summarised as a series of steps that are not difficult for young children to learn:

1. preparation, establishing ground rules and consent of all to participate

2. telling perspectives, each in turn, on the problem

3. dialogue to help each to understand the other's perspectives and underlying interests

4. brainstorming to suggest possible solutions

5. facilitated negotiation (revisiting steps 1-4) to assess, synthesise, and choose a solution

6. affirmation of the agreement, planning follow up, closure.

Peer mediation is commonly used and often effective in schools across North America and elsewhere (Jones, 2004). However, where implementation support is inadequate, programmes are not always sustainably institutionalised, or 'mediation' may be reinterpreted into older, less democratic forms of monitoring by high-status peers (Bickmore, 2001). Mediation works best where the parties have equivalent status, because a mediator has limited authority to ensure that less powerful participants are not re-victimised. There is substantial debate, for example, about whether and how it can be used in cases of sexual harassment. Mediation is under-utilised as a process for facilitating thoughtful deliberations about academically relevant subject-matter in classrooms.

Peacemaking circle practices, especially those rooted in North American and New Zealand (Maori) aboriginal traditions, have become increasingly popular in restorative justice contexts and in schools (Amstutz and Mullet,

2005). There are various circle processes in use, including a group con-ferencing model with Maori roots (Moore, 2003). My preference is a talking-piece process which has North American aboriginal roots (Pranis *et al*, 2003).

There are many types of talking circles, be they for sharing, creative inven-tion, support, and dialogue on controversial issues, or for restorative justice peacemaking and problem-solving. A talking piece is passed se-quentially, so that every participant has an opportunity to speak and be heard, or to pass on the talking piece without speaking. Participants in-clude not only the direct parties to the conflict but also supporters for each one and representatives of the larger community affected by the conflict. This helps balance power differentials and so enables peacemaking circle processes to confront even power-imbalanced and serious harm situa-tions.

A main goal of a peacemaking circle is to repair and strengthen com-munity relationships. The facilitators ensure before the meeting that each participant enters the circle voluntarily and well-prepared for the process, then in the meeting they ask a sequence of open-ended questions that each participant has an opportunity to answer. Although every circle is different, these questions typically invite participants to describe and understand the problem and the consequences of harmful actions and to probe the causes and options for addressing the problem, generally shar-ing experiences from similar situations. Although circles are often used for sharing in classrooms, they are under-utilised as processes for addressing escalated conflicts including identity-based discord and controversial issues.

Complex conflict cases: incorporation of conflict learning opportunities in curriculum

The other way to develop conflict management capacity emphasises not conflict *resolution*, but conflict *education* – foregrounding in classroom lessons the problems and conflicting viewpoints that give each subject meaning. Here it is important to ensure that activities are focused on learning, not on winning. It is equally important to design learning pro-cesses that enhance equity, so they do not implicitly reinforce intolerance or the silencing of less powerful participants.

Many potentially controversial issues don't seem controversial when they are aired in class: mainstream views may be unconsciously reinforced because they are *not* explicitly questioned. For example, most literature and history narratives implicitly embed gendered and heterosexual assumptions and silences. Assumptions about sexuality and gender roles are embedded unconsciously in representations of 'wives' and 'families,' and in choices about which stories and social policy questions matter (Bickmore, 2002a). Gender identities and intimate relationships are immensely important concerns for young people, so deliberation about such roles and discourses could make the curriculum especially engaging. When a middle school teacher guided her English/social studies students in their observational study of gender roles and air time in other classrooms, a number of formerly quiet female students 'spoke up passionately throughout our discussions – some for the first time' (Schur, 1995:147). Asking conflict analysis questions such as whose interests are represented here, whose voices are present and absent, has the power to transform uncritical assumptions into opportunities to learn about areas of potential controversy.

Some official curriculum objectives do explicitly invite practice with analysis and dialogue about various social and political conflicts (see Bickmore, 2005a). For example in Ontario, Canada, social studies expectations for children aged 11 to 12 include 'identify current concerns of Aboriginal peoples (eg self-government, land claims)'. Units for students aged 12 to 13 includes one on conflict and change, including 'analyse and describe conflicting points of view about an historical event (eg the expulsion of the Acadians), giving examples of fact and opinion'. Students aged 15 to 16 are asked to describe the origins and rationale for social support programs such as pensions, unemployment insurance, and medicare, and to 'assess their effectiveness in meeting the needs of various segments of society'. In Manitoba, Canada, students are required to 'recognise bias [and] discrimination and propose solutions' including issues such as relocation of Native People on to reserves, comparing and contrasting past with present reserve life and how one might help to 'reduce the disparities and human rights violations ... [in] internal and international disputes'.

However, such human rights issues are not simple disputes, and should not always be handled as if they embodied two equally valued sides. Roger and Wendy Simon (1995) argue that students should learn to recognise and perform consciously the 'social act of retelling' such 'risky stories' about tragedy and violation, so that they become capable of taking responsibility for naming certain stories as important, for making decisions about what to include and how, and consequently for helping to build a more just and peaceful world. William Kreidler (1990) offers strategies for revising debating activities to incorporate role reversal and consensus-building elements, in order to ensure a focus on listening and investigating toward understanding and on deliberation, rather than reinforcing closed-minded or uninformed viewpoints. Thus controversies may be aired as constructive conflict learning opportunities.

Conclusion

Building peace requires taking risks, but *not* addressing pressing global and local problems is also risky. In the short run, it makes school curriculum irrelevant and disengaging, and in the longer run, it doesn't build citizen capacity to solve the problems upon which our lives depend.

> Shielding children from global problems cannot be a solution to preserving their sense of hope. ... [Young people] already know from television that many people lead wretched lives because of environmental degradation, armed conflicts and poverty, and that some adults are not hopeful about change. ... [If] children hear little acknowledgement of these realities, they conclude that educators either do not care or are not being honest. ... Youth need to theorise about possibilities. (Werner, 1997:250-251)

Young people and their teachers are likely to remain hopeful and effective when they have guided practice and encouragement to handle meaningful conflicts in interpersonal interaction and in academic curriculum areas.

Teaching and learning with conflictual issues should be grounded in key principles and practices for peace building, such as distinguishing problems and interests from symptoms and actions, thoughtful communication, and responding both creatively and critically to the choices conflicts present. In particular, gender- and culturally-sensitive perspectives help to highlight the essential elements of strengthening relationships, equity and inclusive process that are crucial to a sustainable peace building approach to conflict. Teachers need support for risky teaching so that they can effectively help all our students to become powerful peace building citizens.

References

Amstutz, L. S. and Mullet, J. H. (2005) *The Little Book of Restorative Discipline for Schools: Teaching Responsibility, Creating Caring Climates.* Intercourse, PA: Good Books

Bickmore, K. (1999) Elementary curriculum about conflict resolution: Can children handle global politics? *Theory and Research in Social Education*, 27 (1), pp45-69

Bickmore, K. (2001) Student conflict resolution, power 'sharing' in schools, and citizenship education, *Curriculum Inquiry*, 31 (2), pp137-162

Bickmore, K. (2002a) How might social education resist (hetero)sexism? Facing the impact of gender and sexual ideology on citizenship, *Theory and Research in Social Education*, 30 (2), pp198-216

Bickmore, K. (2002b) Peer mediation training and program implementation in elementary schools: Research results, *Conflict Resolution Quarterly*, 19 (4)

Bickmore, K. (2004) Discipline for democracy? School districts' management of conflict and social exclusion, *Theory and Research in Social Education*, 3, 2 (1), pp75-97

Bickmore, K. (2005a) Foundations for peacebuilding and discursive peacekeeping: Infusion and exclusion of conflict in Canadian public school curricula, *Journal of Peace Education*, 2 (2), pp161-181

Bickmore, K. (2005b) Teacher Development for Conflict Participation: Facilitating Learning for 'Difficult Citizenship' Education, *International Journal of Citizenship and Teacher Education*, 1 (2), www.citized.info

Fisher, R., Ury, W. and Patton, B. (1991) *Getting to Yes, second edition*, New York: Penguin Books

Galtung, J. (1996) *Peace by Peaceful Means: Peace and Conflict, Development and Civilization,* London: Sage Publications and International Peace Research Assn.

Hargreaves, S. (1997) Peace education: Politics in the classroom? In R. Case and P. Clark (Eds), *The Canadian Anthology of Social Studies*, pp 109-121. Burnaby, BC: Faculty of Education, Simon Fraser University

Harris, R. (2005) Unlocking the learning potential in peer mediation: An evaluation of peer mediator modeling and disputant learning, *Conflict Resolution Quarterly*, 23 (2), pp141-164

Jones, T. (2004) Conflict resolution education: the field, the findings, and the future, *Conflict Resolution Quarterly*, 22 (1-2), pp 233-267

Kreidler, W. (1990) *Elementary perspectives: Teaching concepts of peace and conflict,* Cambridge, MA: Educators for Social Responsibility

Kumashiro, K. (2004). *Against Common Sense: Teaching and Learning toward Social Justice,* New York: Routledge

Lederach, J. P. (1995) *Preparing for peace: Conflict transformation across cultures.* Syracuse: Syracuse University Press

Merelman, R. (1990) The role of conflict in children's political learning, in O. Ichilov (ed) *Political socialization, citizenship education, and democracy*, pp47-65, New York: Teachers College Press

Moore, D. (2003) *Community conferencing for young people in conflict.* www.mediate.com

Pranis, K., Stuart, B. and Wedge, M. (2003) *Peacemaking Circles: From Crime to Community.* St. Paul, MN: Living Justice Press

Sadker, M., Sadker, D. and Klein, S. (1991) The issue of gender in elementary and secondary education, *Review of Research in Education*, pp269-334

Schur, J. (1995) Students as social science researchers: Gender issues in the classroom, *Social Education*, 59 (3), pp144-147

Simon, K. (2001) *Moral Questions in the Classroom.* New Haven: Yale University Press

Simon, R. and Simon, W. A. (1995) Teaching risky stories: Remembering mass destruction through children's literature, *English Quarterly*, 28 (1), pp27-31

Slee, R. (1995) Adjusting the aperture: Ways of seeing disruption in schools, in R. Slee (ed) *Changing Theories and Practices of Discipline*, London: Falmer Press

TDSB (2003) *A Teaching Resource for Dealing with Controversial and Sensitive Issues in TDSB Classrooms*. Toronto: Toronto District School Board

Torney-Purta, J., Lehmann, R., Oswald, H. and Schultz, W. (2001) *Citizenship and Education in 28 Countries: Civic Knowledge and Engagement at Age 14*. Amsterdam: IEA (International Assn. for the Evaluation of Educational Achievement)

USIP (2005) *Guide to Using Simulations*. www.usip/org/class/guides.html

Vibert, A. and Shields, C. (2003) Approaches to student engagement: Does ideology matter? *McGill Journal of Education*, 38 (2), pp221-240

Werner, W. (1997) Teaching for hope, in R. Case and P. Clark (eds) *The Canadian Anthology of Social Studies*, pp249-253, Burnaby, BC: Faculty of Education, Simon Fraser University

Wilson, E., Hass, M., Laughlin, M. and Sunal, C. (2002) Teachers' perspectives on incorporating current controversial issues into the social studies curriculum, *International Social Studies Forum*, 2 (1), pp31-45

School linking: a controversial issue

Fran Martin

School linking is currently being promoted by official bodies and NGOs in Britain. However as Fran Martin discusses in this chapter, uncritical acceptance which fails to problematise the relationship between schools may perpetuate patronising attitudes. Following a detailed exploration of how linking may reinforce negative prejudices towards the South she describes a case study where schools in the North avoided these difficulties, and are developing a mutually supportive relationship.

First you came to us as missionaries, then you came to us as colonisers, now you come to us as linkers (Conference participant, 2002, cited in UKOWLA, 2006)

Introduction

School linking is usually considered to be uncontroversial and a 'good thing'. In this chapter I question this and show how our attitude to linking reflects our general attitudes to education, the alleviation of poverty and active citizenship. My aim is to problematise an area normally perceived as uncontentious and illustrate the controversial nature of linking. Thus the purpose of this chapter is not to act as a guide to school linking but to examine the factors that affect linking and in so doing help teachers avoid developing links that 'come dangerously near to epitomising a new form of colonialism which endorses the traditional stereotype of the dependency of people in the South and the exploitative nature of western culture' (Disney, 2004:146).

Why is school linking a controversial issue?

A recent small-scale study investigated the preconceptions held by some Year 2 pupils about The Gambia. The school in which the study was conducted had a long established link with a rural primary school in The Gambia, so the pupils already had some experiences of life there through activities such as exchanges of work, studying the country in geography lessons and fund-raising. Their ideas contained the usual stereotypes – *it is hot, their houses are made of mud, they have straw roofs, they wear rags, they have nothing to wear on their feet* – some of which could be attributed to things seen on television – *they have skinny tummies; I've seen that on adverts* – but there was also evidence that the school link activities were a factor in this negative stereotyping:

> T: What about the children in Gambia, what do you think the children are like?
>
> P5: Hmm. Well, not that happy because they don't have many toys to play with so they have to make them.
>
> P4, P2, P1: Operation Christmas!
>
> P1: Yes! We gave them toys. I sent a Noddy car.
>
> T: You sent a car?
>
> P1: Yes a Noddy one.
>
> .....
>
> P3: For Christmas, every single Christmas, we get boxes and put paper on it and then put toys in it and send it to Gambia.
>
> P2: Operation Christmas Child.
>
> (Martin, 2005: 47)

For me, this research (Baskerville, 2005) exemplifies why school linking, particularly between schools in mainly rich countries in the North and mainly poor countries in the South of the world, is controversial. It raises all sorts of questions such as

- Why did the school want to establish a link?
- Why did they choose to link with a school in rural Gambia?
- What did the school hope their pupils would learn from the link?
- Is this the sort of learning that appears to be taking place?
- What is the relationship between learning that is happening as part of the link, and learning that is happening in other contexts such as TV?

- Why is 'Operation Christmas Child' part of the link when The Gambia is a predominantly Muslim country?
- Is involving pupils in charitable actions appropriate as part of an educational venture?

All these questions are interlinked and how any individual responds to them will be affected by their ideological stance and the value judgements they might make about issues such as charity, power relations, north-south economic inequality and the nature of the contact between the linked schools. This starts to become controversial when there are differences in ideology; differences which will occur *within* a school or country as well as *between* schools or countries.

How different ideologies and values affect school linking is discussed under two main headings: The impetus for linking, and Learning from linking.

The impetus for linking

There are strong driving forces for school linking, each providing its own cultural and ideological context. Those that are most influential are the educational context, political context and teacher dispositions. Linking brings these contexts and their ideologies together and this is where some of the tensions begin.

Educational context

The aims and purposes of the National Curriculum for England are a combination of providing opportunities for pupils to learn and achieve, and promoting certain values that prepare them 'for the opportunities, responsibilities and experiences of life' (DfEE/QCA, 1999:10-11). It was perhaps for this reason that citizenship and PSHE were added to the revised curriculum, setting out the knowledge, understanding and skills required for pupils to 'play an active role as future citizens and members of society'. This emphasis on playing an active role is, I believe, one of the things at the heart of controversy over school linking.

What does it mean to play an active role? Although the requirements for the citizenship curriculum are provided by the government (DfEE/QCA, 1999), the interpretation varies according to people's educational ideology. Halstead and Pike (2006: 34-40) have identified three alternative but not mutually exclusive aims for Citizenship Education:

- to produce informed citizens
- to produce committed, active citizens
- to produce autonomous, critically reflective citizens.

The first focuses on providing information about citizenship. The second also aims to 'encourage moral and social responsibility and community involvement' (*ibid*, p35). As well as developing knowledge and concepts, it emphasises promoting the values and dispositions inherent in society. A criticism of the second aim is that it could lead to passive citizens who re-inforce, but do not have the skills to be critical of, the *status quo*. The third aim, however, brings an essential critical dimension in which the rights and responsibilities of one group are weighed against those of another and where considerations of social justice and human rights are central to any decisions for action. This is endorsed by Halstead and Pike (2006:40) who maintain that 'a fundamental aim of Citizenship Education is to pro-duce critically reflective citizens who participate in political debate and discussion and who campaign actively for change where appropriate'.

It is not uncommon for schools that link with a school in the South to fund-raise and send gifts to support their partner school. Action of this kind reflects the aim of producing committed, active citizens, but does it encourage them to be critically reflective?

Political context

In 1997 the British government published its White Paper on International Development. The impact of this on education has been seen in various publications (DfES, 2004; DfES/DfID, 2005) which identify school linking as one of a number of strategies for achieving a global dimension in the curriculum. Speaking at a secondary head teachers' conference in 1999, Clare Short, then Secretary of State for International Development, said that while wanting

> ...every school in the country to have the opportunity to develop a link with a school in the South ... linking is an area which needs great care. I am not interested in links which are one-sided, or which are based simply on charity because they do not create mutual respect and learning. But where links are based on equality and mutual learning, and on a genuine commitment from both sides, the results can be remarkable. (cited in Mackintosh, 2007)

Clare Short's views support a critical, reflective approach to citizenship. However, there are other driving forces which complicate the issue and perhaps help explain why many schools offer some sort of charity as part of their school link. Part of the UK's International Development strategy is to achieve the Millennium Development Goals, of which poverty reduction is first on the list. It is evident that education is seen as one of the key means of achieving these goals and that the formal education sector has a crucial role to play (DfID, 1999). From a political perspective I might therefore ask: how can I help reduce world poverty? From an educational perspective I might ask: how can I help pupils understand the causes of poverty *first* and use this understanding as a basis for *their* deciding how they might help to reduce world poverty? This is how I interpret Halstead and Pike's aim of producing 'autonomous, critically reflective citizens' (2006: 34).

Along with powerful educational and political drives, teachers' personal dispositions affect decisions about whether to link, who to link with and what action to take when difficult issues arise.

Teacher dispositions

Teachers need to feel personally motivated to take part in a school link. In addition, teachers' world views – their assumptions, beliefs and values – will have a profound impact on that link. In a North-South school link, teachers in the Northern school will at some point have to consider how they will respond to economic poverty and, quite possibly, to requests from the Southern school for financial support. How one responds is controversial. The table below provides some of the arguments for and against

The case for aid	The case against aid
Aid acts as an expression of humanitarian concern and provides people in the developed world with a channel through which to direct that concern	Aid creates dependency by making weaker governments or countries dependent on stronger ones, thus putting them at a disadvantage in economic or political discussions
Aid acts as a limited but effective means of redistributing global wealth	Aid distorts the free market, which is the most important engine of growth, as has been shown in the past history of the now developed world

The case for aid	The case against aid
Aid can help developing country governments to provide vital development infrastructure and planning e.g. roads, water and sanitation, planning services and education.	Since 'we' are the givers and 'they' are the receivers, aid can promote attitudes of superiority and reinforce racist attitudes. Aid reinforces stereotypical images
When properly administered and used, aid can help those most in need by providing emergency assistance as well as help with long-term development in areas such as health, education and human rights	Aid is used to divert attention from other more important issues such as trade, debt and the role of transnational companies which have much greater and often negative impact.
Aid is a mechanism whereby the experience and expertise of the better off parts of the world, are made available to the poorer parts	Aid is currently used for economic, political and strategic reasons and is thus aimed at maintaining the current character of world inequality rather than challenging it
(Regan, 2002:127)	

aid which could equally be applied to schools thinking about responding with charity.

Challenging the practice of giving aid is an extremely sensitive area. Firstly there is enormous resistance in schools where it questions the established practice which makes one 'feel that you are doing something good' (UKOWLA, 2006). Secondly, there is some evidence to suggest that 'Southern schools regularly see resource gain as one of the positive expectations and results of a school link' (Fricke, 2006). In other words, the current global political and economic systems support aid as a response to poverty and it takes courage, underpinned by strong principles, to challenge this *status quo*.

Learning from linking
The discussion above suggests that school linking has the potential to be controversial because of the varying demands of educational, political

and personal agendas. In some respects there is a goal that all would agree to – the ultimate reduction of world poverty. However, the means by which this goal might be achieved will differ and this is where clarity about the educational reasons for linking is essential.

What do we hope pupils will learn?

If, as proposed, linking is best seen within a context of an education which seeks to develop autonomous, critically reflective citizens, then the most appropriate sources available for identifying learning objectives are arguably those which focus on citizenship (DfEE/QCA, 1999), the global dimension (DfES/DfID, 2005), and a combination of the two (Oxfam, 2006). The aim is to develop pupils' understanding of key concepts such as diversity, social justice, human rights, interdependence, sustainable development, conflict resolution and values and perceptions. Oxfam be-lieves that such understanding will enable pupils to contribute to 'secur-ing a just and sustainable world in which all may fulfil their potential' (Oxfam, 2006:1). One might question whether a school link, with all its complexities, is the most appropriate means of achieving these objectives. As Temple states:

> A school link isn't essential to developing your pupils as global citizens, it's only one of a whole range of ways you can do this. ... School linking shouldn't be developed simply to tick the box marked 'global citizenship'. (Temple, 2006:14)

Teachers' willingness to engage with and question their own assumptions and values about global development issues is fundamental to good prac-tice in school linking (Martin, 2005). Even where teachers are willing, the learning takes time and is profoundly affected by different cultural expectations. A colleague who has led student and teacher study visits to The Gambia for a number of years is the first to admit that she made mis-takes based on cultural misunderstanding.

> Often a [Gambian] school had a room labelled 'library', some provided by aid agencies or European community groups. We had been asked for more books, so groups were encouraged to take story books with them, to give to the schools. It was disheartening to see in the library [on sub-sequent visits] rarely, if ever, used piles of dust-covered books. Talking these experiences through with Gambian friends, we learned important lessons. The books were nearly all culturally inappropriate for nursery and primary pupils, explicitly European with nothing African. White people doing things beyond children's understanding and experience, in

unfamiliar nuclear family groups rather than in extended families. Pictures of totally unfamiliar plants, animals, places and things, and stories beyond the children's comprehension. It's only from the upper primary years that pupils can read English. Schools have no mechanisms, or staff, to implement a library system. We discovered that the people most interested in reading these books, and for whom they were most appropriate, were those who had left secondary school and who wanted to maintain their English. They were also the ideal people to read and explain them to younger children. So we have learned to give books to someone in the village, for the local youths and children to come to their compound, for different age groups to look at the books there, under the shade of the mango tree. (Mackintosh, 2007)

For all the perceived advantages of linking with a school overseas, there are clearly also disadvantages. Some educators are now advising that a link between schools in contrasting physical and cultural environments within the UK would be a better starting point and would achieve similar results in terms of pupils' understanding as global citizens (Drake, 2006).

What do pupils actually learn?

In the school at the beginning of this chapter the teachers were dismayed at what the children appeared to be learning from their school link. It seemed to be directly contrary to their intentions. What might account for this disparity?

While it is reasonable to expect that the educational aims of each school in a successful school link will be compatible, research indicates that learning is particularly useful when, among other things, participants have *incompatible* value-sets (Scott, 2005). This is one of the real benefits of intercultural learning: that it offers opportunities for teachers and pupils alike to challenge their prejudices and reassess their world views, as my colleague did over her years of visiting The Gambia. Nevertheless, it is a mistake to assume that intercultural contact will automatically lead to learning of this type. Younge (2005) observes that although common sense suggests that the more contact you have with different peoples, religions and ethnicities, the less potential there is for stereotyping and dehumanising those different from yourself, 'even that small achievement depends on the quality and power dynamics of the contact'.

Some research shows that, because of a mixture of the influence of our world view (Gaine, 1995) and the ways in which we conceptualise the 'other' in cross-cultural experiences, cultural exposure can reinforce rather than challenge stereotypes. For example, contact which focuses on differences rather than similarities in the human condition is more likely to lead to pupils developing negative attitudes towards the distant or contrasting place and its people (Wiegand, 1992). Whereas, if activities focus on similarities between the partner schools and their pupils, positive attitudes and a sense of connection are more likely to be fostered. But this approach is not without its drawbacks. Disney shows how, where schools did focus on similarities, there was some indication that

> ... the children's estimation of the worth of their peers in the partner school is affected by the extent to which they possess modern consumer items ... Teachers may also latch onto this, as it is a much more comfortable image with which to work. ... We cannot afford to dismantle some stereotypes and [simply] replace them with others. (Disney, 2004:145)

A focus on similarities and connectedness might therefore be counterproductive to the aim of becoming critically aware of the social and political structures that support inequalities, if that was where it ended. However, if a sense of connection were established before thinking about differences and the reasons for them, pupils might begin to understand how they could take action that would challenge the *status quo*. Lee advises that intercultural programmes 'might need to focus on providing not only the opportunities but also the instructional support for the students to understand how differences are constructed' (2006:212).

This all serves to illustrate how the interrelationship between factors affecting school linking can be complex. The following section describes how one school is grappling with these complexities.

School linking as positive action

Somers Park Primary School in Worcestershire has an active three-way partnership with Chumbageni Primary School, Tanzania and The Key School, USA. It is part-funded by the Department for International Development (DfID). The UK school website states that 'the primary aim of the group is to develop a strong ethos of the global village for the pupils of all three schools, creating a strong channel of communication between pupils to deliver understanding of differing and shared beliefs, values and concepts' (www.keyschool.org/education/staff/staff.php?sectionid=266).

The key concepts referred to in the core objectives are citizenship, interdependence and sustainability. Teachers from the three schools have met – in Tanzania and the UK, with a planned visit to the USA in 2008 – to discuss their visions for the development of the partnership and have identified a range of activities that will form part of the link. These visions are, in summary, characterised by:

- regular, confident and persistent communications between lead staff at each school to plan, regulate, monitor and audit developments and relationships
- visits between the three schools whenever possible, to facilitate conferencing
- various forms of communication between pupils of similar age groups to help build long term relationships with partners in each school
- exchanges of artefacts, images, flags, maps and symbols to be displayed in each school and used as teaching aids
- a dedicated area in each school – a display board, artefact table, zone or class area – that symbolises and celebrates the links
- each school to incorporate the study of the localities of the other two within their geography, history or PSHE programmes
- sustainability as a significant part of discussion and linked work
- tree planting (figure 1) at all three schools, symbolising the life force of the link and contributing to the local microclimate. Schools to communicate their strategies for improving the sustainability of their schools. This will form a vital theme of conferencing
- each school promoting the work of the partnership in the surrounding community, promoting the objectives of the triangle and seeking support in achieving the schools' goals and their good practice.

Figure 1

Somers Park School has identified the types of learning that they believe will be of value to their pupils as follows:

- knowledge   of cultures different from ones own
- awareness   of the needs of others and that our actions impact on others
- empathy   with the challenges that face those living at subsistence level
- positive attitude to undertake action to good effect, meeting an objective
- cognitive skills   reflecting our culture in the light of another

No school link is perfect, but as the headteacher of Somers Park says, they are learning all the time and the nature of the partnership evolves accordingly. For example, the school and community have been involved in raising funds which have been used to develop a computer centre at Chumbageni to facilitate regular communication. Is this an example of charity or of facilitating a link? How would the children in each school see it? The schools continue to grapple with the issue of charity versus equality.

The schools re-thought the purpose of linking. They looked beyond charity and exchange of information to a more meaningful link in which they were learning equally from each other. Sustainability then became the heart of the partnership. This clear conceptual focus, underpinning all linking activities and relating to each school's overall educational aims, has affected the curriculum at Somers Park School. During a visit to Chumbageni, teachers learned how the Tanzanian School had created a vegetable garden for which the pupils were responsible, a patch allocated to each class. The produce was used by the school and the wider community. Thus, through active participation, the pupils learned how they could contribute to the sustainability of their community.

Somers Park School adapted this idea to suit their own context. As well as a Global Garden (figure 2) which is the joint responsibility of Year 6 and Reception children, the school is developing other sustainable practices such as composting areas (figure 3) for grass cuttings and food waste. This is having a positive impact on teachers and parents, who are now composting more of their organic matter at home, a success that has been shared with the partner schools.

Figures 2 and 3

Final thoughts

This chapter shows that school linking is not simply a 'panacea ... to fulfil the global dimension and citizenship requirements' (Young, 2006:11) and other demands made by government. Fricke observes that 'the linked schools, teachers and students involved in a link find themselves in very different circumstances: environmentally, culturally, historically, politically, economically [and] educationally' (2006:12) and all this will influence why schools seek to link, what activities are deemed appropriate as part of the link, and what is learnt from the link. I have focused on just one aspect of school linking, economic disparity, as a means of illustrating how the factors cited by Fricke (above) interrelate and cause real dilemmas for schools. There are no easy answers to these difficult and controversial dilemmas, but if teachers are unwilling to engage with them, 'school links can quickly become educationally meaningless' (Fricke, 2006:21). However, when thinking is based on mutuality and equality, and incorporated in a global citizenship curriculum, school linking can be exciting and enjoyable for all involved. In the school referred to at the beginning of the chapter, the teacher went on to address some of the negative stereotypes described.

> The children in my class began by actually believing that 'Gambian people hunt for their food or they will have nothing to eat but rice'! I wish you could have seen their faces when they saw some of my images ... displayed on an interactive whiteboard – they make a real impact. I've heard comments like 'Oh! They wear clothes!'. ... There is so much for them to see and learn and they are loving it. (Baskerville, personal communication)

Acknowledgements

My thanks to Ben Ballin of the Teachers in Development Education (Tide~) Centre in Birmingham with whom I co-led a study visit to The Gambia 2002-2005, which has contributed significantly to my thinking about global partnerships.

References

Baskerville, S. (2005) How does teaching and learning at Key Stage 1 challenge children's misconceptions of distant people and places? Unpublished dissertation in part fulfilment of a BA in Primary Education, University of Worcester

DfEE/QCA (1999) *The National Curriculum: Handbook for primary teachers in England,* London: HMSO

DfES (2004) *Putting the World into World Class Education.* London: DfES

DfES/DfID (2005) *Developing the Global Dimension in the School Curriculum.* London: DfES

DfID (1999) *Building Support for Development: DfID Strategy Pape*www.dfid.gov.uk

Disney, A. (2004) Children's Developing Images and Representations of the School Link Environment in Catling, S. and Martin, F. (eds) *Researching Primary Geography, London: Register of Research in Primary Geography*, pp139-147

Drake, M. (2006) *Successful Global Awareness in Schools: developing and consolidating the global dimension, a handbook for teachers.* Lancashire: Global Education Centre

Fricke, H-J. (2006) North-South school linking: a review of approaches. Unpublished report commissioned by Plan UK

Gaine, C. (1995) *Still No Problem Here.* Stoke-on-Trent: Trentham Books

Halstead, J. M. and Pike, M. A. (2006) *Citizenship and Moral Education: Values in Action.* London: Routledge

Lee, M. M. (2006) Going global: conceptualization of the 'other' in interpretation of cross-cultural experience in an all-white, rural learning environment, *Ethnography and Education*, 1 (2), pp197-213

Mackintosh, M. (2007) Making Mistakes, Learning Lessons, *Primary Geographer*, 62, pp19-21

Martin, F. (2005) North-South Linking as a Controversial Issue, *Prospero*, 14 (4), pp47-54

Oxfam (2006) *Education for Global Citizenship: A Guide for Schools.* Oxford: Oxfam

Regan, C. (2002) *80:20 Development in an Unequal World*, Co. Wicklow and Birmingham: 80_20 Educating and Acting for a Better World in partnership with Tide~

Scott, W. (2005) 'ESD: what sort of decade?' Keynote address at the UK launch of the UNESCO Decade for ESD, December 13th

Temple, G. (2006) Global Citizenship: Thinking about linking, *TES Teacher*, March 31, p14

UKOWLA (2006) www.ukowla.org.uk/ accessed 26 July, 2006

Wiegand, P. (1992) *Places in the Primary School: Knowledge and Understanding of Places at Key Stages 1 and 2.* London: Routledge

Young, L. (2006) *A Good Practice Guide to Whole School Linking.* Nottingham: MUNDI

Younge, G. (2005) Please stop fetishising integration. Equality is what we really need, *Guardian*, September 19

Speak no evil, see no evil: the controversy about saying 'hate' in mainly white classrooms

Manju Varma-Joshi

Living in a predominantly white province in Canada, Manju Varma-Joshi draws on her research about the nature and prevalence of racist abuse suffered by people from minority ethnic backgrounds. Though the subject matter is New Brunswick, her diagnosis and her prescriptions are relevant for mainly white communities elsewhere. She indicates how communities which define racism in terms of extreme acts are able to deny the abusive and racist nature of everyday acts such as name calling. Varma-Joshi questions the reliance on multicultural education and celebration of diversity to counter racism. She offers a number of strategies to challenge racism in the classroom, starting with students' existing knowledge and experience.

In 1971 Canada led the world in converting multiculturalism from concept to policy. Since then, it has strengthened its commitment to ethnic and cultural diversity with a series of policies and laws that support the Multicultural Act. These include nation-wide policies such as the Canadian Charter of Rights and Freedoms (1982), the Canadian Human Rights Act (1985), the Employment Equity Act (1995) and the Immigration and Refugee Protection Act (2002). Canada has reinforced its commitment to diversity by signing international conventions including the Universal Declaration of Human Rights and the International Covenant on Economic, Social and Cultural Rights. Various departments of the Federal government either produce antiracist education materials themselves or provide grant money for research in the area.

In Canada, education is a provincial responsibility. For their part, provincial departments of education have incorporated a multicultural perspective in varying degrees as part of an overarching philosophy or a distinct component in various curricula. This certainly paints a positive picture, and an initial glance suggests that multiculturalism is working well in Canada and her schools.

However, all may not be as it seems. This chapter draws mainly on three recent antiracist education research projects in which I have been involved, conducted in New Brunswick, a predominantly white Canadian province. The earliest study (Varma-Joshi, 2000) involved a class of twenty-eight students aged 10 to 12, Twenty-six were identified as white, one was Chinese born and another Canadian born and Jewish. This critical ethnography examined how children who live in predominately white locations perceive Canadian identity.

Our second study (Varma-Joshi *et al*, 2004) took a different focus. We interviewed visible minority youth on their perceptions of racism. A compelling result of this project was our participant makeup. The majority of our participants was either of African descent, indigenous Black or Aboriginal. We were left wondering why we had no participants from other visible minority groups. Did they not experience racism? Did they perceive racism differently? Were they reluctant to come forward? We attempted to answer some of these questions in our final study (Baker and Varma-Joshi, 2006). We broadened our focus by contacting visible minority youth in two cities of different provinces (New Brunswick and Ontario) and questioned them about their *interactions* with their mainly white peers, not just about experiences of racism.

In both these studies, participants related various experiences of overt racism. Indeed we found considerable racism in the white population, mirrored in the schools, despite the rhetoric of the Acts and multicultural education policies. Central to this was a reluctance on the part of whites to acknowledge ethnic and racially based hostility. Any attempt to identify racism was characterised as erroneous, melodramatic or violent. The white people preferred to concentrate on benign celebrations of cultural diversity and ignore discussion of racism. Thus the controversy lies not so much within discussion of racism but at the more basic level of definition, recognition, acknowledgement and identification.

Why is racism in mainly white areas of Canada a controversial issue for schools?

Despite the rhetoric of an integrated multicultural society, all is not well. In the mainly white areas of Canada, it is controversial to suggest that much taken-for-granted behaviour is racist. It is controversial to try and bring racist abuse into the open, and teachers, students and ethnic minorities in these communities who try to speak out about such racism may find that they are treated as the problem, potentially ostracised and silenced. Consider this: a few years ago I was scheduled to speak at a local university about my research into racism. The morning of the presentation, I received an anonymous letter attacking my research as 'fear mongering'. The final sentences of this short letter read 'New Brunswick is fine the way it is. Leave it alone.' In the safe environment created by the forum, I presented the letter to the audience and used it as a point of discussion. There were people there who said they agreed with the letter writer but were afraid to speak out for fear of being called racist. In this instance, instead of silence and pretence, the voiced fear was a springboard for discussion.

Perhaps the reason that discussing racism in a mainly white classroom is controversial is because it demands that white people look beyond their normal line of vision. As Miller (1997) points out in his article 'Breaking the Silence', 'members of majority cultures are so accustomed to seeing themselves reflected everywhere they look, that they take it for granted that their values, beliefs and expectations are universally accepted' (p260). Discussing racism forces predominately white communities to question that which is taken for granted. It demands that we be critical and creative.

No racism here?

As in Britain and the United States, a common myth in most predominately white locations in Canada is that racism is a problem of the big cities where the majority of ethnic minority people live (Gaine, 2005; Lewis, 2001; Varma-Joshi, 2000; Jones, 1999). In Canada, this misconception is nourished by the way racism is defined and popularly understood as involving blatant and violent acts (McIntosh, 1990). In New Brunswick and other predominantly white areas, such violence is relatively rare, so racism is perceived to be a minor problem. The result is that whites tend to discount or trivialise intolerance and name calling, even though the victims of racism themselves identify racist name calling as common, abusive and hate-filled. Research indicates that complaints about racist name calling of this type are often played down or not followed up by principals and teachers. For example, one subject in our study hit a classmate who had made a racial slur, and was told by his principal that name calling 'didn't justify me hitting him because being called a nigger is no different than being called a geek or a nerd' (Varma-Joshi *et al*, 2004).

In Britain, institutional racism and name calling are increasingly recognised as part of the spectrum of racism in which violence is at the extreme end (Macpherson, 1999). New legislation such as the Race Relations Amendment Act (2000) has done much to ensure that racist language is not tolerated and official material from the DfES explains clearly why such name calling is abusive and unacceptable (http://www.standards.dfes. gov.uk/ethnicminorities). Nonetheless there is still evidence of low level racism in mainly white communities and the continuing myth that the 'problems' lie elsewhere (Gaine, 2005).

Denying the seriousness of racist abuse is in part the consequence of believing that active strategies against racism cause or intensify the problem. In her *Letters to Marcia* (1985), Canadian educator Enid Lee noted, 'Raising the topic might be compared to breaching a code of conduct. Some of us believe that the more we talk about racism the worse it becomes. The implication is that if we don't talk about it, it will go away' (p6). Apparently, if we see no evil and speak no evil, such evil ceases to exist.

If only it were that simple. For example, many local citizens in New Brunswick refused to acknowledge that a recent case (2000) where a burning cross was erected in the front yard of a black immigrant's home, and the perpetrator publicly made racist comments in court, was indicative of a larger social problem. Sadly, the general denial of a racist incident simply mirrored an authority response. Initially the attending police and the legal system were unwilling to describe the incident as a hate crime. Instead, it was described as vandalism. It was only after a public outcry by the local multicultural association that the charge changed to inciting hatred.

This mute-blind approach was evident in several of the New Brunswick schools we visited. During a conversation with one of the superintendents, I expressed concern about the absence of a policy dealing directly with overt racism. He explained that policies regarding race relations existed under the heading of student 'health and welfare', a statement claiming that every student has the right to a safe and healthy environment. When I asked about policies to deal with racist behaviour, the superintendent replied, 'We have no such policy; we don't like to flag these issues' (Varma-Joshi, 2000).

Where racism is acknowledged, the perpetrators' responsibility may be defused by blaming the victim. For example, some of our participants attempted to get redress for racist experiences in school, and instead of receiving help many were made to feel that their plight was of their own making. One male student exclaimed, 'They [teachers and principal] say, 'You just want attention, you're just saying that, you're using this...you're always using color as an issue' (Baker and Varma-Joshi, 2006). A First Nations female participant recalled a guidance counsellor asking her, 'What did you do to agitate the kid to call you that name?' (*ibid*).

Multicultural education's focus on disclosing racism has also led to accusations of divisiveness. Neito (1994) echoes this tendency: she identifies the way schools avoid 'bringing up potentially contentious issues in the curriculum in fear that doing so may create or exacerbate animosity and hostility among students' (p403). Attitudes like this support the belief that discussion about systemic racism, past racist policies and recognition of personal injustices, will not only divide students but may even incite violence. Yet the result is neither peace nor unity but rather ignorance and disempowerment. Effective multicultural education wages war against the latter reality by presenting students with the lessons from our racist past and the strategies to recognise and attack present-day prejudices. Racism is confronted not in order to lay blame or provoke deeper hatreds, but to encourage empathy, perspective taking and social peace.

Complicity and deflection – denial of the power relationships

Blaming visible minorities and avoiding discussion about racism in school tactically directs the conversation away from another controversial issue – white complicity. We cannot explore historical or present-day racism without interrogating the role played by white society. This means admitting that whites benefit from racism and that racism is caused by overt hatred and is nourished by covert silence. In her article, 'White privilege: unpacking the invisible knapsack' Peggy McIntosh (*ibid*) outlines how whites have the privilege of being able to avoid thinking about racism, while visible minorities do not. Her contention is that if we are to truly fight racism, we need to explore how one group benefits while another suffers. In schools, the refusal to delve into such issues is disguised as a misdirected attempt to avoid making children feel uneasy – or justified as benefiting black children. Teachers believe they should take a colour-blind approach, and they claim to treat everyone the same. Many cling to the 'celebrating diversity' model, focusing on cultural food and festivals.

Since Jonathon Kozol's famous indictment of racist education 40 years ago (Kozol, 1967), many educators have spoken out against the misconception that avoidance effectively protects children from the ugliness of racism (Neito, 1990; Banks, 1998). While it may appear that teachers are doing their students a favour, the reality is that it is more for the benefit of the teachers. I would go further, and argue that avoiding acknowledging and tackling racism in schools is more about the ideological position in our general society than about the welfare of students. After all, curricula are politically contrived documents that say more about what a society wants children to learn than what they *should* learn.

In the post 9/11 world, avoiding dialogue and relying on stereotypes is particularly dangerous. Although media reports and much of the research has focused on the challenges faced by Muslims and Arabs living in large urban settings, such groups in smaller, predominately white locations also report experiences of racism. In a recent study, Baker and Tanaka (2005) spoke to Muslims and Arabs living in New Brunswick about their post 9/11 experiences. One participant remarked that he sometimes did not reveal his background because 'You could see the change in the eyes of people looking at you if they knew you were an Arab or a Muslim' (p22). Others talked of suddenly finding themselves the object of fear. For example a respondent who sells large rugs described how a police car stopped in front of his business; the policeman explained that they had received an anonymous call saying he was moving bombs. The participant assumed that the complainant had seen rugs being moved in and out of his business premises. As another participant said, 'We became in one day a potential threat'(*ibid*, p23).

Bringing racism into the open

In this climate of ignorance and denial, teachers need to bring racism into the open. However, this can backfire, as Sara, a Jewish teacher who took part in my research discovered when she discussed her ethnicity and experience with her 10 to 12 year-old students

> I used to do a unit on racism; you know, really talk about hate and all of the horrible things that have happened because of hate. But it upset too many parents.... They thought it might bother the students. When I argued for it then everyone was saying, 'oh it's because you're Jewish; you guys always want to talk about racism.' I wanted the children to talk

about racism because I want them to learn how to deal with it. And yes, because I'm Jewish. I know what can happen if you ignore hate. But no one wants to know about that kind of hatred. It's just easier to forget. (Varmi-Joshi, 2000:127)

Even Sara's attempts to report racism were discouraged –

[Once on Meet the Teacher Night] a lady came to the door. I asked her to come in and she said, 'No thanks. I just wanted to see what the Jew looked like.' I have walked into my classroom and found swastikas on my board, I have been called a dirty Jew. I've reported all of this but I was very politely told that I shouldn't try to cause trouble. Well I will cause trouble if it means bringing racism into the open. (*ibid*, p94)

Young participants in a recent research project also demonstrated that they clearly understood the controversial nature of speaking up. When asked about racist experiences, many of our participants spoke about 'being nice', a strategy that involved respecting the teacher, working hard and ignoring racism (Baker and Varma-Joshi, 2006). In one case, a black female participant actually discouraged a black teacher from discussing racism in the classroom because she feared that it would cause discord in the school (*ibid*, 2006). Rather than learning to deal with controversial issues, these students, many of whom were newcomers of less than five years residence in Canada, had already learned what topics were better avoided.

Multicultural education: can it address racism?

Following the introduction of multicultural policies and curricula guidance, many of the ethnic minority participants in the studies hoped that multicultural education would offer a solution to racism. They felt they were perceived as a threat partly because many white New Brunswickers knew little about their cultures. Participants in our study wanted schools to dispel some of the stereotypes that abound about Muslims and Arabs. However, they complained that schools wanted to keep control of such teaching. For example, one woman offered to come to her child's classroom and give a talk about her culture, but her invitation was never accepted.

The critique of multicultural education, however, went deeper than a desire to see cultural stereotypes dispelled. The collective assertion from our minority participants was that white New Brunswick students are not only unaware of minority cultures living in their province, but have no sense of the racism such groups experience. Educators familiar with the situation agree that the problem is not ignorance about festivals or specific cultural practices, but white students' unfamiliarity with the lived realities of ethnic minority people (Baker *et al*, 2000).

Tackling racism through classroom practice

How should we bring discussion about racism into the classroom when we know it is a minefield of controversy? As one young teacher once asked me, 'What do I do if I want to discuss racism in my class and the school is against it? I live in this community and I want to stay here.' A good question.

First, a teacher needs to start with simple scenarios. While it is tempting to go to the larger global issues, to do so without first providing students with simple examples from their own experience and communities can lead to confusion and even entrench existing stereotypical beliefs. Despite my caveat that multicultural education and celebration of diversity cannot ever be sufficient in tackling racism, it can provide starting points.

A simple exercise that I do with my university teacher training students examines the length to which they are willing to go in order to accommodate difference. While it is easy to claim personal accommodation of difference, actually to do so is usually more complicated. Each year, my students learn this first hand through a class assignment that examines the school calendar. I introduce the assignment with the comment that the current school calendar is closely related to the Christian calendar. Most, if not all, of my students agree and sometimes identify Christian-based school holidays. I then give my students a list with twenty holidays based on different ethnic groups' special days. Placing them in groups, I ask them to create a school calendar that allows for ten holidays and reflects Canadian cultural diversity.

This task always makes them uncomfortable. However, it also generates interesting discussions about how far majorities and minorities should accommodate one another. In the debriefing session, students discuss how they chose their holidays and the difficulty they had with the process. Some express surprise at their own reluctance to change the calendar; others are shocked by the resistance of others in their group.

What is especially interesting is that minority participants' perceptions, revealed in the research projects about the importance of background knowledge, seems to be vindicated. Students who do this exercise after experiencing some input about other cultural groups employ different strategies than those who do the exercise as an introduction to the pedagogy. However, it is not so much knowledge about other cultures as familiarity with the pedagogy of multicultural education that seems to be effective. Good practice in multicultural education – as in teaching about controversial issues – involves working in a spirit of 'community of enquiry', setting ground rules for debate, respectful attention to different points of view and so forth (Claire, 2004, chapter 4).

Students who have experienced good practice in multicultural education ask questions about the different holidays, weigh their importance against each other and display a deeper level of reasoning in devising their calendar. They exhibit the thoughtful accommodation that effective multicultural education helps to promote. This group is also more likely to have a completed calendar by the end of class! In other words, the exercise is not only about learning to accommodate difference on a macro level by providing space to different ethnocultural groups; it is also about learning to listen to the diverse opinions within their own group. The pedagogy of teaching controversial issues is all-important. It is pointless and usually self defeating to lecture or moralise to students. Rather, they must be given the opportunity to debate in small safe groups, where each person's voice can be heard, including those of the minorities who may otherwise practise self-silencing, or be silenced by others.

Teachers who wish to discuss racism in their classroom need in the first instance a good understanding of a multicultural pedagogy. But there is more to it. Passionate commitment to social justice and equality will be essential for the teacher, but not sufficient. In order to challenge the controversial issue of racism in the classroom teachers need a sound understanding of what racism really entails. Teachers, and through them students, need to know about the spectrum of racism, with casual and often taken for granted name calling at one end, through stronger abuse and acts of violence, to institutional racism which keeps the whole power structure in place. They need to understand that racist name calling is not like calling someone a nerd, and thinly masks contempt, disrespect and even hate. Racism is a word laden with history, culture and emotion.

From simple to complex – addressing the controversies and the complicity

Familiar work on festivals which leads into discussion about accommodation of minorities can be a powerful way into tackling controversy, involving moving from the simple to the complex. While it is important to talk and learn about the social aspects of our different cultures, it is even more important not to end the conversation there. Students need to acquire the tools and language to critique the ways in which difference is treated in our society. They need to learn to think about and question power relationships and complicity. They need to consider who gets included and who gets left out. And most importantly, they need to learn to ask why? My students have the opportunity to ask such questions when we discuss the curriculum guides. Most are familiar with a curriculum guide. They understand that they are official documents which they, as teachers, are legally bound to follow. However, their knowledge often falters when I ask them who creates the curriculum. They tend to guess the government, the schools or the universities but seldom know for sure. I raise levels of awareness by asking 'who gets to decide what goes into the curriculum? How are these people chosen? Who is not chosen?' They may be discomforted but they start to see that the curriculum is not simply a document of instruction, but one reflecting power and privilege.

We also discuss how differing perspectives can influence the teaching of the curriculum content. My example is a popular topic in Canadian history – the building of the railroad. All my Canadian students are familiar with the story of how the railroad united our nation from east to west; they know the names of the great engineers that Canadian history has elevated to heroes. I then point out that everyone in the story is white and that most are men. This is how the history of the railroad is generally presented. Then they learn about the Chinese railroad workers who were brought from China, forced to pay a head tax, given the most dangerous jobs and then denied the right to settle in Canada once the railroad was completed. My aim is for students to appreciate that the curriculum is interpreted through particular lenses, and that there are gaps and biases in what is included.

Racism in a white world

We need to teach students about racism in their own communities and not just racism in another time and another place. Even in mainly white groups, there will be experience of racism, probably at second hand. A powerful way to address this and students' possible complicity is through mining their own experiences. I often ask students to write about a personal experience of racism, for example, directed at some other person or group. I ask if they have ever heard a racist joke. I want my white students to begin to think about the complexity of racism, and that it is not just about overt acts of hatred against others, of which they are innocent. Soon students are sharing stories about the uncle who spews racist beliefs at every family dinner, the Asian student from high school that everyone assumed was good at maths, the neighbouring First Nations community that they have always feared and so on.

While this activity does give my students insight into racism, this does not come easily. Firstly, having me, an East Indian woman, as their professor, often makes them imagine that they have to write something extraordinarily compelling, something that will impress me. In their post-activity journal entries many of my students report that this would have been an easier assignment if I were white. Students often say they feel stressed about saying the wrong thing or misinterpreting an experience as racism when it was not. They also write about not wanting to insult me or appear racist themselves. They are surprised to hear that I am feeling uncomfortable too, teaching about racism. I talk to them openly and honestly about the dilemma of being a visible minority antiracist educator. I discuss a white teacher's position of privilege in being able to discuss racism without appearing self-serving.

Such discussion is also problematic for my white students since few have ever questioned their access to and enjoyment of power and privilege. Conversations become even more heated when they realise that in order for others to enjoy privilege and power, they themselves will have to give something up. While they are often willing to allow for privilege-sharing through expanding the resources, for example, creating *more* teacher education opportunities specifically for visible minority students, they are reluctant and sometimes even infuriated by privilege-sharing with fixed resources, for example, keeping the same number of teacher education places, but assigning some specifically for visible minority students.

The assignment is also stressful because later, I ask my students to question their own complicity in the examples of racism they have offered. Were they directly involved? How did they react? Did they participate? Then we move to even more difficult questions. For example, I ask how many students agree that inaction in a racist incident is in itself racist behaviour[1] – even in the case of something as apparently innocuous as a joke. By no means everyone agrees. Indeed, many students attempt to justify their inaction or disparage 'political correctness', which they claim unreasonably condemns all behaviour as potentially racist. Many argue that it is not their fault that racism exists and that their white skin does not make them liable for all behaviour exhibited by other whites.

Conclusion

Teaching controversial issues does not have to be a negative experience. It is through discussion of controversial issues that we learn to think critically, judge arguments, weigh evidence, recognise differing points of view, form and defend thoughtful opinions and articulate our positions. Students also learn that not everything has a right or wrong answer and that differing opinions can co-exist.

Challenging racism forces predominately white communities to question that which is taken for granted. It demands that we be critical and creative. If we see no evil and speak no evil, we lose opportunities for growth and development.

When racism is conceived as acts of hate rather than unchallenged beliefs, little can be done to counter or contest racist convictions. Although certainly not bigots, my students appear to belong to the group whose minds have been formed in a racist society. Does this mean that their actions are not detrimental to Canadian society? This question is best answered by Sara, the Jewish teacher who invited me to work in her classroom after showing me a racist pamphlet distributed in a New Brunswick city (Varma-Joshi, 2000). The pamphlet called for support for 'ridding Canada of Jews, Niggers, and gays ... in a holy war for a white Canada'. Putting down the pamphlet and looking me straight in the eye, Sara talked about how her white students draw Canadians:

> Those drawings are quiet and unintentional echoes of the overt messages stated by full force bigots. This is what is in those drawings, the white Canada that this racist pamphlet calls for. The bigots want a white Canada because they think it's the way Canada should be. My students draw white Canadians because they have been taught the same norm. Ask a student in my class can a Canadian be black or brown and they will say 'oh of course'. But when they reveal their true beliefs, they draw a white Canada. And this puts a fear in my heart. (Interview, February 14, 2000)

It also puts fear in mine.

Note

1 I have also asked this question before the described assignment and most students have always agreed that inaction was racist. The responses become more mixed when applied to a situation where the students are themselves involved.

References

Baker, C. and Tanaka, C. (2005) From Invisible to Visible Minority: The Aftermath of 9/11 for Muslims in New Brunswick. Unpublished study

Baker, C. and Varma-Joshi, M. (2006) Sweetening the Tea: Immigrant Youth Interactions with White Peers. Unpublished study

Baker, C., Varma-Joshi, M. and Tanaka, C. (2000) Sticks and Stones: Racism as Experienced by New Brunswick Youth, *Canadian Journal of Nursing Research*, 33 (3), pp87-105

Banks, J. (1998) The lives and values of researchers: Implications for educating citizens in a multicultural society, *Educational Researcher*, 27 (4), pp4-17

Claire, H. (2004) *Teaching Citizenship in Primary Schools*, Exeter: Learning Matters

DfES Ethnic Minority Achievement Site (England and Wales) http://www.standards. dfes.gov.uk/ethnicminorities

Gaine, C. (2005) *We're all white thanks: the persisting myth about white schools*. Stoke-on-Trent: Trentham Books

HMSO (2000) *The Race Relations Amendment Act*. Her Majesty's Stationery Office

Jones, R. (1999) *Teaching racism or tackling it?* Stoke-on-Trent: Trentham Books

Kozol, J. (1967) *Death at an Early Age: The Destruction of the Hearts and Minds of Negro Children in the Boston Public Schools*. New York: Houghton Mifflin

Lee, E. (1985) *Letters to Marcia*. Toronto: Cross-Cultural Communications Center

Lewis, A. (2001) There is no 'race' in the schoolyard: Color-Blind Ideology in an (almost) all-White school, *American Educational Research Journal*, 38, pp781-811

McIntosh, P. (1990) White privilege: Unpacking the invisible knapsack, *Independent School*, 49 (2), pp31-36

Macpherson, W. (1999) *The Stephen Lawrence Inquiry Report*. Cd 4262-1, HMSO

Miller, H. (1997) Teaching and learning about cultural diversity: Breaking the silence, *The Reading Teacher,* 51 (3), pp260-2

Neito, S. (1990) Affirming Diversity: The Sociopolitical Context of Multicultural Education, New York: Longman

Neito, S. (1994) Lessons for students on creating a chance to dream, *Harvard Educational Review*, 64 (4), pp392-426

Varma-Joshi, M. (2000) Multicultural children's literature: Storying the Canadian identity. Unpublished doctoral dissertation, OISE/University of Toronto

Varma-Joshi, M., Baker, C. and Tanaka, C. (2004) Names will never hurt me? *Harvard Education Review,* Summer, pp175-208

Key strategies for teachers new to controversial issues

Bernadette Dean and Rahat Joldoshalieva

Bernadette Dean and Rahat Joldoshalieva address the challenge of teaching about controversies in an educational climate which has little tradition of encouraging dissenting views. They provide a detailed description of the approaches which a group of practising teachers doing an MA first learned about and practised on their course and then took into their own classrooms. Although the approaches were local and national, the overarching issues of concern to young Pakistani children and their teachers are clearly similar to those elsewhere. And the strategies are transferable to other countries and contexts.

Introduction

Democratic citizenship requires understanding and thinking about ways to address societal issues, most of which are controversial. How do we inspire young people to think about controversial issues such as child labour or global warming? It is hard enough to do this in countries with a history of democracy; it is an even greater challenge in newly practising democracies. This chapter reports on work with students aged 10 to 14 who tackled topics such as the Kashmir issue, child labour, the Kalabagh Dam and deforestation in social studies classrooms in Pakistan. The issues raised and strategies used are relevant to teachers in all countries.

Since its creation in 1947 Pakistan has tried to institutionalise democracy. In an effort to develop and sustain democracy, power was devolved to the districts in 2002. District government facilitates greater citizen participation in decision making, as more citizens stand for office, participate in elections and oversee the government. If citizens are to play their role effectively at both local and national level, they must be educated for citizenship. However, in Pakistan, citizenship education has been criticised for preparing Pakistani children only to parrot what is written in government prescribed textbooks rather than to act as democratic citizens who are knowledgeable about controversial issues at local, national and global levels (Nayyar and Salim, 2004; Dean, 2000, 2005).

Dealing with controversial issues in the classroom is a generic problem, seldom made explicit in countries which pride themselves on their democratic principles. Pakistan provides a different case, which allows us to examine hidden ideologies determining how citizenship is taught. The lessons from this case study are thus relevant to all teachers struggling to find effective ways to teach about challenging issues.

The Social Studies course

In order to prepare social studies teachers to educate for democratic citizenship, the teaching of controversial issues was incorporated into the Masters of Education Programme (MEd) at the Aga Khan University-Institute for Educational Development (AKU-IED). This programme aims to equip teachers with the knowledge, skills and attitudes required to improve the quality of education in their schools, so that they can prepare students to act as democratic citizens and transform their society. The social studies course facilitators strongly believe that the task of social studies education is to develop informed, active and responsible citizens. To be skilled and competent citizens, students need to feel empowered, know and value their own potential for positive action and use it to address the issues and problems encountered in their society. This requires the study of contemporary issues and draws on all the disciplines of social studies: developing a wide range of skills such as information gathering and processing, critical thinking and communication skills; and fostering dispositions towards tolerance, risk taking and diversity, justice and equity. Eleven teachers from the MEd class of 2007 opted to take the social studies course. The course ran over two semesters, each eighteen weeks long. Eight weeks were allocated to teaching about controversial issues. At the start of the course the teachers' practices and views about teaching controversial issues were explored.

The teachers' views and practices

The majority of the teachers had not taught controversial issues specifically but had dealt with them as they emerged in classroom discussions. Secondary school teachers claimed that it would be possible to teach controversial issues in their classrooms if they were trained, whereas primary school teachers felt that this might not be possible with younger children.

Most of the controversies identified by the teachers were global political issues affecting Muslims, such as the Iraq war, Iran's nuclear programme, the anti-Muslim media and the Palestinian-Israeli conflict. A few national issues like the Kalabagh Dam and Kashmir were also considered contentious. Issues they faced daily in their classrooms, schools and neighbourhoods, such as decisions about where students should sit in the classroom, what topics to teach and the medium of instruction, were not recognised as controversial, though it is interesting that when children were asked what they thought was controversial, they did include issues that affect their everyday life in school.

The teachers identified a long list of challenges but only two positive possibilities. The challenges included

- the emphasis on curriculum coverage
- preparation for examinations at the expense of all else
- absence of controversial issues in textbooks
- perceptions that controversial issues are too sensitive to discuss in the classroom
- fear of repercussions given the narrow vision of school heads and the larger community
- a culture that prohibits expression of contrary opinions and arguments
- fear of creating conflict between students
- teachers' lack of knowledge or skill to deal with contentious situations.

However, the teachers identified the training they expected in the social studies course as offering increased knowledge about controversial issues and acquisition of the strategies and skills required to teach them.

Preparing teachers to teach controversial issues

We identified four stages to address the teachers' needs. These are relevant for anyone learning to teach about controversial issues. The stages are:

- identify and research the background to a controversial issue
- create a means of sharing findings, eg a web-blog
- clarify meanings and the nature of the controversy through discussion
- understand a range of strategies to deal with controversies in the classroom.

To help teachers with the last two stages – appropriate discussion and strategies – they were introduced to four strategies for the classroom:

- discussion
- debate
- role play
- demystification

Discussion

Discussion skills are not innate. The students' age, knowledge and interests should be considered in selecting and preparing who is to lead discussion about a controversial issue and whether it is to be done by a student or the teacher. Effective discussion skills encompass three stages: preparation, management and evaluation. Establishing an open discussion climate is a prerequisite for conducting effective discussions as students must feel free and secure to share their views and argue with each other. The teacher's role is to act as a moderator to ensure that diverse and competing perspectives are fairly heard, to ask questions and challenge ideas, eg by playing devil's advocate. Where controversy arises over values, teachers should help students identify, interpret and clarify their values. Finally the discussion itself should be summarised and evaluated collaboratively by the teacher and students.

Debate

This requires reasoning skills, analysis of multiple relationships and consideration of multiple perspectives. Students learn to organise their ideas, present their opinions clearly and support them with facts using the conventional formal debate structure of speaking for and against a motion, without necessarily taking a vote at the end. The teacher's role is to judge and assess the process of the debate and the quality of arguments presented. Teachers need sound knowledge of the topic so they can deepen students' understanding of the concepts and issues.

Role play

This involves learning through acting and observing. During role play participants examine their own feelings, attitudes and perspectives as well as those of others, and develop self-understanding and empathy. Role play can facilitate problem-solving, communication and social skills (Blatner, 2002). When students take control, they draw on creativity and imagination. Effective role playing follows four steps: preparation, introduction, enacting and monitoring. It is important to follow up role play with discussion. Non-participant students can play the role of engaged audience and join in the discussion that follows the role play.

Demystification

Demystification requires extensive knowledge of the issue, plus critical thinking skills and open mindedness. The strategy differs from discussion in that existing arguments are analysed, whereas in discussion, arguments are generated.

There are four steps to this strategy (Clarke, 1992):

- *What is this issue about?* The nature of the controversy is identified: namely what information, concepts and values underpin it.
- *What are the arguments?* What is the content of the argument? Is the position taken valid? The criteria used to judge validity can either be moral or prudential. Moral criteria are concerned with how everyone will be affected, and prudential criteria with how myself and my group will be affected.
- *What is assumed?* The assumptions behind the argument are identified and evaluated on the basis of who is making the argument.
- *How are the arguments being manipulated?* What information has been selected and emphasised or ignored.

The strategies in practice

Using global warming, a subject which the participants themselves offered as an example of a controversial issue, we can see how the group learned to manage conflict through practising some of the strategies they had learned.

First, the group was encouraged to recognise that controversies such as this have several facets: whether the phenomenon exists at all; what has caused the phenomenon; what would be desirable outcomes to intervention; what interventions might be appropriate. A reading *Is global warming a myth or reality?* was used as part of the *demystification strategy*, with teachers identifying the arguments, assumptions and manipulative strategies. This was followed by learning skills to handle controversy, namely 'disagreeing in an agreeable manner' and 'respecting each other's ideas'.

When the group had used the demystification process to assess the issues and practised skills to deal with the controversies identified, they moved to the question *Is global warming a natural phenomena or a result of human activities?* In the ensuing discussion, the teachers sat in a circle. One of us facilitated the discussion while the other recorded the ideas. At times we had to intervene in the discussion to explain some concepts, for example where there were misunderstandings about what the greenhouse effect actually meant. Following the discussion, teachers evaluated their own practice and identified ways to improve.

We then organised a 'Conference of countries on climate change' to help participants learn *role play* strategies. Each pair of teachers was assigned a country – Canada, China, USA, India and Australia – and they were asked to prepare their arguments based on information about the country's position on this issue. At the beginning of the panel discussion, we reminded the pairs to speak from the assigned country's position and not their personal views. It is important that participants in a role play of this nature have time to research the position they are allocated, so that they can enter the spirit of the role play.

Following this introduction and practice, and the participant teachers reflection on their learning, they prepared lesson plans which they taught to pupils in social studies classrooms. Each lesson was followed by teachers' reflection and our critical constructive feedback.

Vignettes of teachers' teaching in the schools

The eleven teachers were sent to four different schools to teach, some to their own schools, others to assigned schools. Each teacher taught three lessons over three weeks. We have selected four teachers' classrooms to show how the four strategies they had learned on the course were implemented.

Demystification

Sadia taught about the Kashmir issue to girls aged 13 to 14, using the de-mystification strategy. The Kashmir issue is essentially the dispute over whether Kashmir is an integral part of Pakistan or India. The issue is rooted in the decolonisation of British India and the creation of Pakistan, which was to be formed from contiguous Muslim majority areas. Pakistan thus holds that Kashmir, with a majority Muslim population and adjacent to areas now forming Pakistan, should be part of Pakistan, whereas India contests that since the Raja of Kashmir handed Kashmir over to India after independence, Kashmir belongs to India.

After eliciting her students' views about how to handle controversial issues, Sadia introduced the social skill of 'disagreeing in an agreeable manner'. She provided a brief background to the Kashmir issue and asked her students to do a 'think-pair-share' activity to identify the controversies.

St1:   When partition took place they were given a choice. The Hindu Raja chose India, but the people are Muslim, so they wanted to be a part of Pakistan.

T: Is it only religious?

St2:   No. It is also about land.

St3:   Power.

T: What do you mean?

St3:   Who has power, they want to show it. India is more powerful.

Sadia summarised the discussion, noting the complexity of the issue. She then distributed handouts about Kashmir; students were required to read this and gather more information from various sources.

In the following lesson students shared their understandings, identified the arguments presented by each stakeholder and the assumptions under-lying them. Sadia then summarised the different arguments. Using examples, she explained what the term 'manipulation' meant and asked students to explain how the arguments were being manipulated.

St1:   Some interest groups hide information from their people to portray wrong images.

St2:   Every party has its own point of view. Indians have theirs and we have ours. In their newspaper, their own perspective is given. If we read our own newspaper our perspective is given.

St3:   The terms which are used are also manipulative, like 'India occupied Kashmir'. This is not what the Indians would say.

T: So then what do you think these manipulations bring?

St 4: Rivalry, dispute.

St 5: Yeah, as a result Kashmiris suffer.

St 6: Yes, India and Pakistan are fighting and Kashmir is the victim.

St 7: It is also bringing competition in nuclear weapons and may lead to nuclear war.

In the third lesson, Sadia asked students to propose solutions. Some students suggested 'peaceful resolution' of the dispute considering all points of view while others considered their group's interests.

St 1: The majority of Kashmiris are Muslims so an Islamic state should be created.

T: Think of Hindus, they are living there too.

St 1: They are a minority; they can be accommodated in any part of India.

St 2: They are also citizens of Kashmir. You can't just ask them to migrate.

St 1: Why not?

St 2: They have their home, business, etc there.

St 1: During partition, many Muslims migrated to Pakistan; when they migrated they left their things there.

T: The Muslims chose to leave India but suppose I am Hindu, I like Kashmir I don't want to move.

St 3: Nobody should force the minorities to migrate.

St 1: It is not migration.

St 2: Now Muslims are in India, they live in peace with Hindus. Hindus can do the same in Kashmir.

The lesson ended with Sadia again emphasising the complexity of the Kashmir issue and encouraging students to be thoughtful as well as critical, and not jump to quick solutions.

Role Play

Rashida used role play to teach girls aged 12 to13 about child labour. In her first lesson she put her students in small groups and gave them photographs of children at work. The pictures showed a very young child asleep over the baseball he was stitching, a young female domestic servant sweeping a house and children working in a brick kiln. They were asked 'What is this child doing? Why is he doing it? What made him do it? Why do you think so? Is what she is doing alright?' Students immediately expressed sympathy for the children, so Rashida encouraged them to analyse the situation. She explained what was meant by a controversial issue and asked how they normally dealt with it. The girls said they tended to argue and finally compromise or break off their friendships, but they thought that boys would get into a fight. Rashida ended the lesson by distributing a handout she had prepared on child labour.

In the next lesson Rashida explained how role play works and asked the students to consider how they could role play the issue of child labour. They suggested depicting a real life situation and a talk show. For the talk show they would have government officials, employers, child workers, their parents and a person who was neutral. She handed out roles to students who had volunteered and gave them time to prepare their positions.

In the following lesson Rashida rearranged the classroom to facilitate the talk show. One group of students performed a role play depicting two children working as domestic servants, in which one gets injured but receives no redress from the employer. The talk show host then invited the 'guests' to share their reactions to the scenario and child labour in general. Finally, Rashida invited questions and comments from the 'audience'.

After the role play Rashida asked students how the issue could be addressed in reality. The students declared that the general public should pay their taxes, that the government should use tax money to provide free education, employers should pay better salaries so parents are not forced to send their children to work. Because they felt they had a moral obligation to contribute to the elimination of child labour they proposed that they should raise awareness of the issue by writing articles or letters to the newspaper.

Discussion

Meenaz asked her Class Seven boys aged 14 to 15, to generate their own list of possible controversial issues. These included the new timetable at school, traffic, child labour and the building of the Kalabagh Dam. The last issue was selected. The building of the Kalabagh Dam is a controversial issue in Pakistan because people living in the province of Sindh are concerned that if dams were built, the rivers would dry up and affect agricultural production which, in Sindh, depends on irrigation. The students had to find out more about the issue and prepare for the discussion by watching the news on television and reading the newspapers.

The next lesson began with the students sitting in a circle and going through discussion skills. The following responses show the quality of their thinking.

St1: We need water and electricity so we should build the dam.

St2: I agree with him. We need to store water as we are an agricultural country.

St6: But Sindh is already receiving less water and if the dam is built it will receive even less. How will the farmers of Sindh cultivate the land?

St10: If the Kalabagh dam is not built there will be a shortage of water and food in the whole country and we would have to import wheat from other countries.

St11: If it is not built Sindh will get water and will grow wheat.

Although students demonstrated some discussion skills, not all were able to make the transition from prudential to moral judgements, as we can see from some Sindhi students' inability to move from support for Sindh's position to a more global view.

Debate

Altynia taught Grade Five children aged 10 to 11 about deforestation, using the debate strategy. She began by teaching the skill 'disagreeing in an agreeable manner'. Then the students were asked to debate the motion 'Should we use wooden furniture?' She chose six students from the class, three to speak for and three to speak against the motion, instructing the rest of the class to follow the debate. Examples from the debate follow:

Speaker 1 FOR: My name is ... My opinion about the motion is that I agree that we should use wooden furniture because it will be difficult to use steel or any other material, for instance if it is a door. Wooden things are comfortable to use in everyday life.

Speaker 1 AGAINST: I am against the idea of using wooden furniture because we will be cutting many trees to make furniture. We will not have shade. Our wooden houses will be burnt easily. ...

Altynia found that she had to repeatedly interrupt students who spoke for too long and she resolved to address this in the next lesson. At the end of this lesson she asked students to summarise what they had learnt and gave them a handout in preparation for the next session when the debate would be: 'Should Pakistan ban cutting down trees?'

At the beginning of the next lesson Altynia checked students' understanding of deforestation and its effects, and clarified issues which were not understood, using the prepared handout. She then again chose six students for the debate and one to act as a judge. The students were asked to prepare their arguments for the next lesson when the debate proper would be held. Altynia tried to avoid the mistakes of the last debate by letting the speakers know exactly how long they had to present their views. After each speaker's presentation, the judge was told to summarise and give the floor to the next speaker.

Speaker 1 FOR: If we cut trees, the birds will die. The animals get extinct....

Judge summarises

Speaker 1 AGAINST: If we ban deforestation, we cannot make furniture and houses. The people who depend on cutting the trees will get poorer...

Speaker 2 FOR: I disagree with him. We can make furniture from metal also and we can make our houses out of bricks.

Speaker 2 AGAINST: But then we cannot have any paper to write on if we ban cutting trees...

Asked to vote for their position at the end of the debate, most students voted to ban deforestation. As well as learning about the different sides to any controversial issue, the children had also learnt about time-keeping, voicing an opinion and the importance of listening carefully. In addition their knowledge and understanding of a controversial global issue had been increased. Using the debate strategy had allowed the teacher to keep careful control and to ensure that both sides were heard.

Is it possible?

The work with the teachers and the results that they produced with students, confirm that it is possible to introduce controversial issues into the curriculum, even in a climate such as Pakistan's which does not encourage dissent from mainstream positions. We concluded that the following factors contributed to the success of the project and offer them as guidelines for others.

Effective training of teachers to teach controversial issues requires:

- specific training for teachers, including discussion about the nature of controversies and training in the use of the strategies described

- teachers taking responsibility for developing their own knowledge about issues so they feel confident to challenge erroneous views or intervene effectively

- teachers planning lessons themselves and trying out the strategies beforehand
- teaching approaches which encourage the active engagement of students, in contrast to didactic approaches to teaching and learning
- support for schools wishing to innovate.

We found that the strategies which worked best in the classroom were those where teachers

- help children understand what a controversial issue is
- teach children how to disagree in a friendly manner
- provide information about the contentious issue in advance of the strategy used
- start with simple issues, possibly from the local community, rather than going straight into the most complex and contentious.

Some positive outcomes of the Pakistani project
The teachers

In Pakistan, as elsewhere, the quality of education in schools depends on the teachers' own knowledge as well as their pedagogic strategies. To ensure quality of teaching, teacher education in Pakistan needs to address both. It is clear that the teachers felt that the project contributed to this goal, and were pleased with their personal learning in areas that were new to them. Moreover, despite initial concerns that they would be accused of indoctrination or lack of patriotism in introducing controversial issues into the classroom, and facing initial hostility from the principal in one school, by the end of the project all the schools were supportive. However, while this verbal support was important, the teachers felt that other school conditions would have to change to facilitate teaching controversial issues. No one was willing, for example, to teach issues relating to religion or sex in the classroom.

The children

The teachers and the researchers monitoring the project noted that children were motivated to learn and developed the skills and attitudes essential for democratic citizenship, including increased confidence. The new approaches provided opportunities to explore and express views and to analyse different perspectives and challenge biased approaches – for example about the Kashmiri situation.

On the other hand, children tended to make claims which they could not support, and lacked knowledge to challenge their peers. Or they rushed to solve problems and make decisions rather than first trying to understand the issue. There was also a tendency to believe that it was the responsibility of the government to address the issues and not their concern. From the point of view of a democratic citizenry, this is worrying.

The training that equipped these teachers with the knowledge and skills to teach controversial issues has shown that this is possible in Pakistani classrooms unaccustomed to such teaching approaches. However, the problems raised by the teachers are universal, and the processes and the strategies identified in the chapter offer a way forward in other contexts.

References
Blatner, A. (2002) Role-playing in Education, Retrieved May 2004, from http://www.blatner.com/adam/pdntbk/rlplayedu.htm

Clarke, P. (1992) Teaching controversial issues: *A four-step classroom strategy for clear thinking on controversial issues*: BCTF/CIDA Global Classroom Initiative 2005 from http://www.bctf.bc.ca/Social/GlobalEd/GlobalClassroom/ClarkePat/TeachingControversiallssues.html

Dean, B. L. (2000) Islam, Democracy and Social studies education: A Quest for Possibilities. Unpublished thesis submitted to the faculty of Graduate Studies and Research in partial fulfillment of the requirement for the degree of doctor of Philosophy, University of Alberta

Dean, B.L. (2005) Citizenship Education in Pakistani Schools: Problems and Possibilities, *International Journal of Citizenship and Teacher Education*, 1 (2)

Nayyar, A.H. and Salim, A. (2004) *The Subtle Subversion: The State of Curricula and Textbooks in Pakistan*, Islamabad: Sustainable Development Policy Institute

Index